Joseph Walter Wilstach

Montalembert

A Biographical Sketch

Joseph Walter Wilstach

Montalembert
A Biographical Sketch

ISBN/EAN: 9783337028275

Printed in Europe, USA, Canada, Australia, Japan

Cover: Foto ©Thomas Meinert / pixelio.de

More available books at **www.hansebooks.com**

A Biographical Sketch.

BY

JOS. WALTER WILSTACH.

NEW YORK:
THE CATHOLIC PUBLICATION SOCIETY CO.,
9 BARCLAY STREET.

Copyright, 1885, JOSEPH WALTER WILSTACH.

PART FIRST.

1810-1835.

YOUTH—TRAVELS—FIRST LITERARY LABORS, . . . 9

PART SECOND.

1835-1857.

PUBLIC CAREER, ... 37

PART THIRD.

1857-1870.

RETIREMENT—"THE MONKS OF THE WEST"—LAST LITERARY LABORS, ... 79

Important Contemporary Events in France.

1810—The Empire of Napoleon, which had reached its acme, was now beginning to lose prestige owing to the successful efforts of the English in the Spanish Peninsula.

1812—War declared by Napoleon against Russia, followed by the disasters of the Moscow campaign.

1814—March 31, Paris capitulated.
Napoleon abdicated in favor of his son and retired to Elba.
May 3, Louis XVIII. entered Paris and was declared king. This marks the beginning of the "Restoration."

1815—March 1, Napoleon left Elba secretly and reached France, and collected recruits for a last effort.
June 18, the battle of Waterloo, in which Napoleon's power was for ever overthrown. He was sent to the island of St. Helena.

1824—Louis XVIII. died. He was succeeded by his brother, the Duc d'Artois, under the title of Charles X.

1830—The Restoration overthrown by a revolution in July, and Louis Philippe, Duke of Orleans, was declared king, and established what is known as the "July Government."

1848—The Louis Philippe régime was overthrown by a revolution, and the king abdicated February 24, and the Republic of '48 was declared under a Provisional Government.
June, insurrection in Paris, instigated by Red Republicans; lasted seventy hours.
Cavaignac appointed dictator.
Louis Napoleon elected president, December 10, for four years, but not to be re-eligible.

1851—December 2, Napoleon effected a *coup-d'état*, gave France another constitution, and was re-elected thereunder.

1852—December 2, Napoleon elected emperor and assumed the title of "Napoleon III., hereditary Emperor of the French, by the grace of God and the will of the people."

1870—July 19, war declared by Napoleon against Prussia.

Part First.

"Je défie qu'on trouve une parole sortie de ma plume, ou tombée de mes lèvres, qui ne soit pas destinée à servir la liberté. La liberté! Ah! je peux le dire sans phrase, elle a été l'idole de mon âme; si j'ai quelque reproche à me faire, c'est de l'avoir trop aimée, aimée comme on aime quand on est jeune, c'est-à-dire sans mesure, sans frein."

MONTALEMBERT,

1810-1835.

IN two cumbrous tomes containing a Latin version of St. John Chrysostom—by their date but seventeen years removed from being *incunabula*—is a prefatory epistle from a bishop of the sixteenth century to the translator of the volumes, from which the name of the translator had been withheld through modesty or some other motive. The bishop expostulates with his friend for the omission and ends with the remark: "If it happen to one walking through a city that he hear the music of a lute behind him, he is seized with a desire to behold the player; so I in reading this book, and knowing it to be a translation from Greek into Latin, have desired to know who was the translator."* If such be the yearnings inspired by a well-done translation, how much stronger and greater are those which are created within us by the works of a great author who has so often filled our minds with the melody of his eloquence! Has any one had his leisure enriched, his imagination fired, his sentiments elevated by the perusal of the writings of Montalembert, and not felt a desire to know the story of the life of him who has left upon so many pages the impress of a noble and generous nature?

---

* "Sicut enim ambulanti per civitatem, si post tergum citharâ personare audiat, cupido incessit videndi quis est ille qui personat; ita legendi hoc opus et e græco latinum factum scienti, quo interprete factum sit" (Preface by Petrus Barrocivus).

He is known to most American readers as the author of the *Life of St. Elizabeth* and *The Monks of the West*. But these incomparable volumes are not his sole claim to renown—without them his name had been famous. As a public man Montalembert has left a deep mark upon his age. He was a leader in his day, first, of the Catholic party under the *régime* of Louis Philippe, claiming in the full nineteenth century the most elemental liberties; then of the conservative elements united under the Republic of 1848 against socialism, communism, and anarchy; finally, in a private station under the Second Empire, wielding his pen and raising his voice in protest against the wrongs of France and those repeated encroachments upon the Papacy which ended in the total confiscation of the Papal States and the centralization of Italy.

I.

Charles Forbes René de Montalembert was born May 15, 1810, in London. His mother was of Scottish descent, his father a French exile. On both sides the family of Montalembert were of distinguished lineage. His paternal grandfather was one of the many *émigrés* of '92 to whom England had opened her ports, and whose *rendezvous* was the house of the illustrious and noble-hearted Edmund Burke. James Forbes, the maternal grandsire of Montalembert, was a man of scientific and literary distinction in his day. Montalembert was born at Mr. Forbes' house in Albemarle Street. Owing to the unsettled condition of European affairs during his childhood he was left for his first eight years in England with his grandfather Forbes, with whom he continued to be an object of tender devotion down to the day of Mr. Forbes' demise, which occurred at an inn in Aix-la-Chapelle, where death overtook the eldest of the party on the way to visit Montalembert's parents. It is to these early associations and the subsequent influence of his mother that Montalembert owed his knowledge of English, which he spoke with the elegance of a native, and which was of much service to him in later years.

In 1816, after the Restoration, Montalembert's father had been named a peer of France and sent as minister plenipotentiary to Stuttgart. Thither Charles was sent towards his ninth year, almost a stranger to his own parents and his brother and sister. Returning afterwards to Paris, the boy made his First Communion, in his thirteenth year, in the church of St. Thomas Aquinas, in the Rue Bac, where forty-seven years later, wasted by the pangs of a cruel disease, he received his last Communion and heard his last Mass. Even before his thirteenth year Montalembert had given evidence of unusual force of character. The records of his diary at this time discover a restless love of study rare in one so young. The eight years spent in the sober light of his grandfather's library, in an atmosphere of books, go far towards accounting for this early bias. At a time when others of the same age were entering with zest into the amusements of childhood Charles Montalembert was pining over the loss of time involved in such occupations.

At the age of sixteen he entered the college of Sainte-Barbe, where he formed his life-long attachment to his friend Léon Cornudet. And here it was that, in a written compact of self-consecration, the two friends bound themselves to their Maker, their country, and to each other, to devote their talents and their powers to God and freedom. Beautiful and consistent beginning of a life made up of unflagging philanthropy and chivalrous devotion to the Church! This remarkable compact was made at the suggestion of Montalembert in his seventeenth year, and is his composition. The seal of this life-treaty was the Holy Sacrament of the altar. Will the Catholic look further for the secret of its fecundity? The noxious influence of secularized schools, which in France have been the main instrument in undermining the faith and morals of her youth and making scepticism the fashion,* left unscathed the heart of Charles Montalembert and the coterie of kindred spirits who, through their whole college course, stood an unbroken phalanx in the storm of infidelity which raged around them.

Political questions had always a great fascination for this youth, whose family had suffered so much from political reverses; and although a diligent student he frequently indulged his tastes in the direction of politics to the detriment of his classical studies. In 1829, therefore, when he left Sainte-Barbe, he went without a prize, imitating in this the school-days of many who, before

---

* On this subject we will quote Montalembert's own words, uttered publicly in 1831 before the Chamber of Peers: " . . . The gangrene has entered these institutions, these colleges, into everything the university has founded, in all that it has protected, wherever it wishes us to place our children and pay to see them destroyed. You know it as well as myself: is there a single establishment of the university where a Catholic child can live in his faith? 'A contagious doubt, a cold and stubborn impiety'—do they not reign over all the young souls whom the university pretends to instruct? . . ." And further on, if more is necessary, he says: "Is not an immorality the most flagrant, most monstrous, most unnatural inscribed in the registers of every college and in the recollection of every child who has passed but eight years there?" (*Discours*, tome i. p. 14).

and since, have become illustrious in the higher walks of life. His days at Sainte-Barbe had had their measure of college vexations; but they marked the beginning of lasting and valuable friendships for a man whose ideal of friendship was ever very high. So that now, as he stood at the terminus of college life and looked back upon the past through the mellow lights of memory, the threshold of the future, concealing behind it the mystery of things to be, stared cold and inhospitable, and he became for a while a prey to that sombre melancholy which is so often the unwelcome appanage of delicately sensitive and poetical natures. Questions, too, at this time as to his vocation very naturally presented themselves; but he came to no conclusion.

From college he went to Sweden, where his father's diplomatic engagements had called him. But this was not a pleasant prospect to him. In the range of frivolous gayeties in which the creatures of a court employ the time Montalembert, although not a cynic, found little or no pleasure. The answered promptings of grace had caused him to set a high value on life. His ardent fancy had conjured up bright visions of substantial success to be gained through the patient and noble processes of self-denial, hard study, and a scrupulous following of his Master. There was nothing, therefore, but vexation of spirit in these occupations, which, according to his rigid code of observation, resulted only in squandering precious time. Breaking as often as he could from court formulas, he divided his leisure between garnering materials for a future article on Sweden and a study of the Catholic philosophers of Germany, to whom the Abbé Studach, a learned and pious priest, had directed his attention. But philosophy was not Montalembert's forte. Politics, but politics in the highest sense, as involving the cause of human rights, was the sphere to which his quick sympathies and restless generosity of soul especially fitted him. Nature had destined him for the heat and anger of conflict. Yet in all his passionate devotion to human rights the cause of freedom and the cause of truth, as revealed by the Master whom he loved, were never disassociated in his mind; and the main struggle of his life was to give the lie to the calumny that freedom and revelation are antagonistic principles.

Montalembert was devoted to the study of Burke and Grattan, the style of the former of whom bears such a close resemblance to the rich profusion of his own. Grattan, "as the unwearied champion of the greatest of causes," says Rio, "soon acquired in the eyes of his youthful admirer the grandeur of the hero of a crusade." O'Connell at this time was waging the cause of Catholic Emancipation. In this contest Montalembert failed not to see the cause of truth and the cause of freedom one. It fired his mind with a consuming ardor. And out of the reading which his interest in Irish affairs drew him into was evolved the plan of writing a history of modern Ireland. His letters and his conversations at this period were of nothing else. And to make his project more feasible he decided to visit the scene of O'Connell's achievements. But this design, which his eager enthusiasm for the cause of his espousal had magnified into the pivotal act of his life, was destined to be thwarted by that intruder who rudely mars so many fair plans; and the history of Ireland, much to the chagrin of its youthful projector, never saw the light. A sister, whose frail health had broken under the stern climate of the North, required his reluctant services as a companion for herself and their mother in the tedious journey of those days back to their home in France, which, however, only two of them ever reached. The sister died at an inn in Besançon.

Nursing the wound of private grief, and not altogether free from a qualm of regret that he had given his services so grudgingly to one whom he had learned to love through the winning agents of gentle manners, he arrived in Paris on the eve of another revolution. His absence had unfamiliarized him with the bearings of French politics, and he was unaware of the coming change. He busied himself, therefore, with his own prospects. After oscillating between the choice of the priesthood and the military service in Algiers he settled finally upon the study of the law. His evenings he devoted to the arrangement of his observations on Sweden in the form of a magazine article. They appeared in the *Revue Française*, after undergoing a pruning operation at the suggestion of the editor, greatly to Montalembert's disgust; after which it was mutilated by M. Guizot, the editor of the magazine, to suit that gentleman's peculiar views of things Swedish. He now began, too, to frequent a social circle where intellectual pleasures were predominant. Lamartine, Sainte-Beuve, and Victor Hugo were among his first acquaintances of note. He also wrote about this time an article on Ireland, and had the mortification of hearing a friend tell him that his Irish dissertation was commonplace and his article on Sweden tiresome. But the humble opinion entertained by him of his own ability made such criticism less unlooked for than the warm approbation with which his father received his effusions.

In July of this year—1830—he at last set out on his much-dreamed-of journey to Ireland. He had not gone further than London when the news of the July revolution reached him. He hurried to France, only to be as quickly sent back to England by his father, who evidently did not set the same value on the presence of Charles at such a time as the young man did himself. Although he exulted at the revolution, there still "lurked a dread in his delight." To one who had in his character as much as Burke or Fox of the power of opposition a triumphant cause had not the attraction which he found in offensive politics. He was an oppositionist, not out of a factious system of criticism, but for the same reason that these two great orators were— because the governments under which they all had to live were far from conforming to their high ideas of justice. His broad humaneness, too, could never lead him throughout his life to dissociate from popular victories the confiscation, the blood, and the rending of dear ties which follow so often in the wake of successful revolution. His own hopes in a pecuniary direction, moreover, were threatened with wreck by the events of Les Trois Jours; for the Montalembert peerage was in imminent danger of revocation. In the state of mind induced by reflecting on recent events and this near possibility of personal misfortune he reached Ireland the year after Emancipation. In the diary which he afterwards published the reader who is curious can see

for himself the details of this young knight's picturesque journey, undertaken out of his devotion to liberty and religion. It would be too much to expect that every trait of the high ideal which fancy had formulated should be borne out by the reality. But to be able to say, as he did, that in the main it was as he had pictured it, is pronouncing an enviable eulogium. He saw O'Connell, shared the informal hospitality of his house, and was present at some of his speeches.* In his travels over the country he familiarized himself with the principal phases of Irish life, social, political, and devotional. At Maynooth he made the acquaintance of Archbishop Murray and Dr. Doyle, of Kildare, who were captivated by his well-directed enthusiasm and the evidences of rare ability displayed by him. He himself was awed and delighted by such company. And we are told that when at the college table one of these gentlemen proposed his health the tender-hearted youth was moved to tears. In September he left Ireland, where he had spent, he tells us, the two happiest months of his life.

II.

During his absence many causes were at work which were to have an important bearing upon the future of

---

* Sixteen years later these two champions of *liberty without bloodshed* were to meet again. But this time upon the soil of France; the older one—"A painful warrior famouséd for fight"—broken in health and hastening to Rome to die upon ground which the martyrs had enriched with their blood; the other cased in the shining armor of great talents, in the mid-splendor of his career, met him as the spokesman of kindred spirits, to address to him such words as are proper on the lips of those who are pursuing a noble course, when uttered to one who has gone before over the same path and left to all who follow the encouragement of his example.

Charles Montalembert. There was forming in France a party, small in number but rich in talent and enthusiasm,

Exigui numero sed bello vivida virtus,

whose object was to regenerate a healthy Catholic opinion in France and seal its union with liberal progress.* The brilliant and unfortunate M. de Lamennais and the gifted Henri Lacordaire were the central figures of this new movement, which had inscribed upon its banners the watchword, Dieu et la Liberté! Montalembert, returning from Ireland, eager for action and pining for a cause, was attracted by this little group. They had formed a society—"Agence générale pour la défence de la liberté"—and set up a newspaper entitled *L'Avenir*, the first number of which appeared October 15, 1830. Montalembert joined the former and passionately devoted himself to the success of the latter. At last he had found an object capable of employing his pent energies. He found with it, too, the man with whom he contracted a friendship which, during the long period of thirty-two years, notwithstanding all the heart-burns and sorrows which such a period can span, all the opportunities which it offered for differences of opinion and misunderstandings, remained ever the same, never tarnished by the rust of suspicion nor weakened by a sense of waning profitableness. From first to last this union was a *medicamentum vitæ et immortalitatis.* "Née au sein des épanchements et des rêves charmants de l'adolescence, elle a survécu aux revers, aux trahisons et aux lâchetés qui ont assombri notre âge mûr."†

* See *Le Père Lacordaire*, par le Comte de Montalembert, 1865, Lecoffre, Paris, vol. iii. of Montalembert's *Œuvres polemiques et diverses*. † Ibid.

That friend was Henri Lacordaire. He had come to Paris in 1822 a sceptic, but a sceptic whose heart was pure and whose idol was liberty. Through the example of edifying associates, such as the celebrated Abbé Gerbet, his heart was opened and the light of truth fell full upon his soul. "A sudden and secret touch of grace," says Montalembert, "opened his eyes upon the nothingness of irreligion.* In a single day he became a Christian, and the next day from being a Christian he wished to become a priest." Lacordaire and Montalembert met for the first time in November, 1830; Lacordaire was twenty-eight, Montalembert was twenty. "He appeared to me," writes Montalembert, "charming and terrible at once, as the type of enthusiasm for the good, of virtue armed for the defence of truth."

After his return to Paris Charles wrote two articles, one on French affairs, the other on England, the last of remarkable sagacity and foresight. Poland, too, occupied his attention in her short-lived paroxysm of resistance, and was the first subject on which he wrote for *L'Avenir*. It was followed by a letter on Ireland. The reader who is curious will find all the articles from his pen which appeared in the *Avenir* by consulting his *Œuvres polémiques et diverses*. The style of these articles is impetuous—passionate declamation in many portions rather than disquisition—yet full of fine thought and creditable observations. Through all the unshackled

* Lacordaire tells us that observation had convinced him that religion was absolutely necessary to the maintenance of human society: "Je suis arrivé aux croyances catholiques par mes croyances sociales, et aujourd'hui rein ne me parait mieux demontré que cette conséquence : La société est nécessaire, donc la religion chrétienne est divine ; car elle est le moyen d'amener la société a sa perfection en prennent l'homme avec toutes ses faiblesses et l'ordre social avec toutes ces conditions " (Letter, March 15, 1824).

élan of these effusions there is a forecast of the splendor which marked the style of riper years.

Shortly after the congenial souls of Lacordaire and Montalembert had come to know each other *L'Avenir* was seized by the Louis Philippe government and MM. de Lamennais and Lacordaire were arraigned. Montalembert was inconsolable that he could not share their lot, regretting, almost with tears, that he had not been a member of the *Avenir* staff. M. Janvier was the advocate of M. de Lamennais. Lacordaire performed with good taste and success the difficult rôle of arguing his own cause. The two journalists were set at liberty, and the *Avenir* enjoyed a triumph. "Lacordaire," says Montalembert, "was not intoxicated by his triumph. On the threshold of his house I saluted him as the orator of the future. But I saw plainly that for him these little vanities of success were less than nothing—mere dust in the night."

In the flush of victory the party of "Dieu et la Liberté" resolved to attack the existing school system—an odious monopoly under the control of the university which precluded the existence of all except government schools. An offspring of the despotism of Napoleon, it had survived both the Empire and the Restoration. Its existence was one of the charges which the enemies of the Restoration had urged against that *régime*. In framing the charter of 1830 they had declared that the existing system of education should be changed "with the shortest possible delay." The *Avenir* now took up the discussion of its tyrannical processes and its evil results. Some recent instances of its odiousness in practice determined Lacordaire and Montalembert to enlist public opinion in the matter. After having presented a numerously-signed petition praying for its repeal, which memorial met with no response, the editors of the *Avenir* announced that, as it was evident the government intended to take no action, three of their staff would open a free unlicensed school in Paris. It was opened accordingly May 7, 1831, by Lacordaire, Montalembert, and De Coux, after a short inaugural address from Lacordaire. On the morning of the second day, while engaged in instructing in elemental matters some poor children of the vicinity whom they had collected, they were all arrested. Of course; and they expected to be. They were brought before the *Police Correctionnelle*. But Montalembert's father had died in the meantime; so, according to the law governing the case, the young peer, with his associates, was arraigned at the bar of the Chamber of Peers. Thus it was, as public culprits, that the two most eloquent men of their day first appeared in the highest tribunal of their country—the one destined soon to startle Paris with a gift of polemic eloquence unknown since the days of Bossuet and Bourdaloue, the other to be the civil leader of the Catholic Liberal party of France through the powers of a brilliant pen and a wonderful gift of oratory. As appreciating better than any one else the cause for the befriending of which they stood under the ban of law, they argued their own defence after their advocate had presented the law-points. Those who had the enviable fortune of being present on this day tell us that the discourse of Lacordaire was manly, strong, and elegant, admirably suited to the occasion and the place—a speech that rolled like burning lava over the objects of his animadversion. Of Montalembert the polished Sainte-Beuve says: "Although a mere youth and a delinquent, his ease and grace, the elegant precision of his style and diction, veiled this fact. . . . The entire chamber listened with a surprise which was not without pleasure to the young man's bold self-justification, and, looking at his talent and grace alone, found in it, first of all, the highest promise of future public service. . . . From that day M. de Montalembert, though formally condemned, was borne in the very heart of the peerage—he was its Benjamin." They were fined one hundred francs (twenty dollars)—equivalent to an acquittal, at least so regarded on all sides. "It was purchasing very cheaply," says Montalembert, "the honor and the advantage of having compelled public opinion to occupy itself with a question vital to our cause."

But the days of the *Avenir* were drawing to a close. The rash and excessive opinions advocated in the journal, but especially those of M. de Lamennais on certitude, had excited the censure of soberer heads in authority. The illustrious trio in the warmth of their convictions, since the question had created considerable controversy among Catholics, determined to appeal to Rome, whither they journeyed in November, 1831. The details of that voyage are familiar to most readers, and we will not attempt to discuss them here.* They led to the closing of the *Avenir*, to the eventual apostasy of M. de Lamennais, to the sore trial of Lacordaire, and threw Montalembert into a vortex of contending doubt and

---

* See Cardinal Newman's *Essays, Critical and Historical*, 2 vols., "Lamennais"; also Montalembert's account in his sketch of Lacordaire above referred to; also Brownson's *Works*, vol. xii.

faith from which he finally emerged in safety. But
there is another phase of this visit to Rome, and a
closely subsequent one, which is not so well known.
Italy's riches in Christian art, which addressed themselves
without effect to the absolute mind of Lamennais, found
in Montalembert a warm devotee. He whose first cry
of admiration had been for a monument of Christian
architecture—the famed cathedral of Rouen—and who
tells us that from the day he met Victor Hugo laboring
upon his *Notre Dame de Paris* he never passed a Gothic
edifice without entering it, was not apt to find unprofit-
able the opportunity of studying in Rome and other
Italian cities their galleries of pictures and their architectural monuments. Their influence was twofold. They
nurtured his faith and strengthened his affections for the
Church, and they fitted him for the task of bringing about
in France, in connection with Rio, a renaissance of
Christian art based upon a healthier and truer sense of
the beautiful, a warmer and purer faith, than those upon
which the Romantic school were founded. The latter
school was poetical and impressionable only. That we
may not be thought too trenchant in this matter, we will
take refuge under the authority of the learned and judicious Foisset, the life-long friend of Lacordaire and
Montalembert. "That which pleased this school in
Gothic churches," he says, "were the recollections they
suggested, the sensation of chilliness (*sorte de frissonne-
ment*) which they caused; the freshness of the vaults, the
twilight of the sanctuary, the secret passages resembling
the labyrinths of the forest—in fine, the picturesque effects of these monuments upon the azure sky. The Empire and the Restoration had passed away without this

school being able to raise itself beyond impressions so miserably superficial." It was not so that Rio and Montalembert looked upon Christian art. With them it had a deeper and a truer meaning, which addressed the heart and not the imagination. For them it was beautiful because in it they saw the embodiment of the Christian faith. And this was a new view in their day and generation. To Rio and Montalembert is due the glory of having established its moral superiority. Its cause occupied Montalembert throughout his life.*

III.

Preceding his companions in their return to France, Lacordaire retired to the country; Montalembert upon his arrival took up his quarters in the Faubourg St. Germain, having, among other friends, such genial spirits as MM. de Coux, Sainte-Beuve, the gifted critic, and Frederic Ozanam, in whose premature death France lost a brilliant scholar, the Church a valiant supporter, and the cause of historic truth an advocate of inspired genius. Speaking of Montalembert at this time, Ozanam says: "M. de Montalembert receives his friends Sunday evenings, when there is a great deal of varied and expansive talk. . . . An odor of Catholicism breathes through these little parties. M. de Montalembert has an angelic countenance and is very brilliant in conversation. He is a

---

* He became after 1840 a member of the Comité des Arts and of the Commission des Monuments Historiques, and so remained down to 1852. He was then dropped from these commissions. Imperialism does not love such talents as Montalembert possessed. His writings and speeches on art have been grouped by him into a volume, *Mélanges d'Art et de Littérature*. We believe there is no English, at least there is no American, edition thereof in our tongue.

good story-teller and extremely well informed. The conversation is animated, the speakers grow excited sometimes, our hearts are **warmed, and** one carries away a feeling of satisfaction and **pure** pleasure, **good** resolutions and **courage for the** future."

From **his** lodgings Montalembert frequently sallied forth on rambles through France, guided **in his** wanderings by the whereabouts **of ancient** churches and monasteries, remnants of **mediæval architecture, whose** defamed fragments and unhallowed **uses drew from him** a lengthy **article, " Du Vandalisme en France," *** where the **indignant protest of a lover of art,** and a Catholic **who** saw the symbols **and** instruments **of** his faith insulted, finds utterance in a resistless torrent **of passionate eloquence, the echo of which is heard thirty years later,** with the **gathered force of** three decades **of study and** experience, in *Les Moines d'Occident*. His *Vie de Sainte Élisabeth* **owes its existence to the chance circumstances** of **an extensive art tour made by him through Germany, as he** himself tells **us in the** brilliant **preface to that** work. **He arrived on** the **19th of November,** 1833, **in** Marburg, **a city** of electoral **Hesse, for** the purpose of **visiting its** Gothic church, **"celebrated not only for its** rare and perfect beauty, **but also because it was the first in** Germany **where the ogee prevailed over the full arch,** in the revival **of art in the thirteenth century."** It bore **the name of St.** Elizabeth, **and it happened that the** day of his arrival was the festal day **of** the saint. **Strange coincidence !** The church **was open, but the melodies, the**

---

* This was addressed as a letter to **Victor Hugo, who** had used a like strain **in** his article, " Guerre aux **Démolisseurs." It is the first** thing in his *Mélanges d'Art*.

anthems, the solemnities of the Sacrifice had not been heard there for three centuries. Its vaulted naves were despoiled and deserted, "but still young in their elegance and airy lightness. Further on, upon naked altars, whence no priestly hand ever wiped the dust, he examined with interest ancient paintings on wood well-nigh defaced, and carvings in relief, all broken, but both alike deeply impressed with the fresh and tender charm of Christian art. . . .

"The stranger kissed the stone hallowed by the knees of faithful generations, and resumed his solitary course; but he was ever afterwards haunted by a sad but sweet remembrance of that forsaken saint whose forgotten festival he had unwittingly come to celebrate." He pursued the study of her life through the libraries of Italy and Flanders. "He successively ransacked those rich depositories of ancient literature which abound in Germany. Charmed more and more each day by what he learned of her," that thought of studying her life became the polar star of his wanderings. Having exhausted the stored lore of ancient libraries, he resolved to visit in person the places she had graced by her presence. "He went then from city to city, from castle to castle, from church to church, seeking everywhere traces of her who has always been known in Catholic Germany as *the dear St. Elizabeth.* . . . Finally he returned to Marburg, where she consecrated the last days of her life to the most heroic works of charity, and where she died at twenty-four, to pray at her desecrated tomb and to gather with difficulty some few traditions amongst a people who with the faith of their fathers had lost their devotion to their sweet patroness."

During his sojourn in Germany, where he was mostly accompanied by Rio, he made the acquaintance and enjoyed the hospitality and conversation of the most brilliant intellects of that country. At Bonn he met the philosopher Windischmann, the jurisconsult Walter, Welcker, the renowned philologist and archæologist, and the theologian Klee, who was at that time one of the three great lights of the Church in Germany. In Frankfort he was graciously received by Madame Frederick Schlegel, the daughter of Mendelssohn. Here, too, he met the painter Veit, whose Madonna he had admired in Rome, and Passavant, the authority of the time in matters of Christian art. In Dresden he was amicably received by Tieck, since Goethe's death the corypheus of romanticism. Here he met Raumer, the historian. In Berlin the jurisconsult Savigny, Gans, professor of law, Madame Arnim (Bettina Brentano, Goethe's friend), Ranke, the historian, and Alexander von Humboldt were among his acquaintances. Here, too, he met Radowitz and attended the lectures of Schleiermacher and Raumer.* In Munich he resided nine months (from December, 1833, to October, 1834), pursuing his artistic studies and cultivating the friendship of such men as Schelling, Döllinger, and Görres.

The elevating effects of such society upon the still plastic character of Montalembert—the refining influences of Germany's rich treasures in paintings, in sculptures, in architecture, acting upon the stores of rich ma-

---

* We could, and probably should, have made the list longer but for the procrustean limits which we have assigned ourselves. At Göttingen he saw the brothers Grimm ; at Stuttgart, Christian Pfister, the historian of Germany, and the critic Wolfgang Menzel ; at Tübingen, the poet Uhland and Möhler, "the prince," says Foisset, "of Catholic theology in the nineteenth century"

terial laid up in his mind by his Italian journeys—can scarcely be overrated. This period was, therefore, by no means the least important one through which his character passed in its stages of development. Can be traced to this epoch those phases of his style which possess a richness of coloring and a perfection of art sufficient of themselves to embalm his works. But, as he has told us above, what guided him through all these wanderings was his design of writing the *Life of St. Elizabeth*. This is well attested by the foot-notes and quotations of that book—so splendid a work of art and of erudition.

His diary of this period—when he had come again to Marburg—gives us a touching picture of Montalembert, racked on the one side by the anxieties occasioned him by the Lamennais *imbroglio*, on the other by an oppressive sense of his own loneliness. His was one of those natures which at all times, and especially under such circumstances as the present, yearn for the sympathy of woman's love—the one element which lacking reduces them to something like supineness. Comparing himself to his friends Rio and Albert de la Ferronays, both of whom were on the eve of happy marriage, he passes upon himself a painful judgment of self-depreciation, calling his life a failure and feeling himself

> ". . . in disgrace with fortune and men's eyes;
> Wishing him like to one more rich in hope,
> Desiring this man's art and that man's scope." *

While pursuing his investigations in the unsympathetic Lutheran quietude of Marburg, oppressed by

---

*. He spoke of his life at this time as "toute finie pour lui—à la fois manquée et brisée."

sentiments of melancholy, who should come to a vision lighting up the night of his sombre thoughts but the old, strong friend—Lacordaire. "He came to me at the tomb of St. Elizabeth to persuade me," said Montalembert. "I was at first displeased with my friend, because he had taken another way from mine and had pronounced himself more publicly and decisively. I was even bold enough to reproach him with his apparent forgetfulness of those liberal opinions with which we had both been set on fire. . . . It was then that my eyes, at first distracted and irritable, but soon, and always after, wet with the tears of everlasting gratitude, penetrated into the very depths of that generous soul" (*Le Père Lacordaire*).

The *Paroles d'un Croyant* had not yet appeared, nor Lamennais' more terrible declaration that his reflection had "led him into grave doubts on many points of Catholicism, and that in consequence he had renounced all priestly functions." When this came Montalembert felt that the Rubicon in this affair had now been reached. On the 8th of December, 1834, after four days' reflection, he sent from Pisa, where we shall soon see him, to Cardinal Pacca a categorical act of submission to both encyclicals. Montalembert had long clung to Lamennais, endeavoring to console and strengthen him under the hardest of all trials to an intellectual man—the censure of his opinions by a crushing authority—urging, beseeching, appealing to him to submit. He had even contributed to his support, and went many times to see him. But finally Montalembert saw what the keener Lacordaire had presaged, and was at last obliged to pen the cruel words which told La-

mennais that henceforth their paths would lie apart—
words not more cruel to him who received them than to
him from whom they were wrung "by the cruel gripe
of a rigid necessity"; for Montalembert must have felt
that he was bidding adieu to a man condemned to a fate
worse than death. But in the company of Lacordaire,
even in the atmosphere of Marburg, everything was
blithe again for Montalembert.

Crossing the Alps as winter approached, Montalembert descended into Italy to join the Ferronays at Pisa.
Here begins the thread of that narrative so beautifully
woven into *Le Récit d'une Sœur*, par Madame Craven
("The Sister's Story," by Mrs. Craven).

In July, 1836, appeared *Histoire de Sainte Élisabeth
de Hongrie*. The success of this work, from whatever
point of view it be judged, was a very marked one. It
has been translated into all the European languages,
and has served, and will continue to serve, as a model
to those who in writing the life of a saint—of one of
those heroic beings who have forbidden to themselves
any of the splendors of this life—desire to see such a
record endued with all the controllable graces of art in
composition and poetry in thought.

"In perusing," said Cardinal Wiseman in reviewing
this book, "the various works which come under our
hand in our duty as reviewers, our feelings must vary
according to their character. We speak not at present
of such as stir up indignant and unpleasant emotions;
the volume before us banishes the thought of all such
from our minds. But in turning over pages of a more
agreeable nature sometimes we may be astonished at the
erudition displayed by the writer; sometimes we may

rather admire his sagacity and genius; some books may convey to us a high opinion of his moral qualities, and others make us long for his acquaintance as a man of amiable and virtuous character. Seldom, however, has it been our lot to experience the peculiar feelings which have accompanied the perusal of the work now on our table—feelings more akin to jealousy than to any other we have described. It was not the research, nor the rich poetical genius, nor the deep religious tone, nor the eloquent language of its youthful author, conspicuous and admirable as all these qualities are, which riveted our attention or secured our sympathy; it was the sincere love, the enthusiastic devotion, with which his task has been undertaken and accomplished that has made us, so to speak, envy him the days and the years which he has spent upon its performance. So pure must have been the heart and soul while occupied with the sainted object of their spiritual affections; so closed must have been the feelings against the rude materialities of life in this sear generation while inhaling the healthy freshness of a greener age; so full of delicious meditation, of varied hope, and of conscious success must his pilgrimage have been. . . . In England it will be probably imagined by many that a peer who could think of writing a saint's life must be a bigot and illiberal, to say no worse. Now, M. de Montalembert is neither: he attaches not the happiness of his country to the augury of a name; he advocates the cause of rational liberty under the government that actually exists, because he considers true liberty as based upon a religious, a Catholic principle, which should predominate under every form of government, and is the inalienable right of every Christian people." *

The book was dedicated by Montalembert to the memory of that sweet sister who died at the inn in Besançon. " Thus," beautifully remarks Mrs. Oliphant—"thus, not like a common book, but like the visionary, poetic revelation it was, it came into the world robed and adorned with the tender recollections of the past and the undefined, passionate, youthful hopes of the future. We have seen a little case with two miniatures which it was Montalembert's custom till the end of his life to carry about with him wherever he went—the portraits of two girlish faces: one over which her early fate has thrown to the spectator a gentle sadness; the other fair and vigorous with the beauty of vitality. The two portraits were those of his sister and his bride. These two fair faces come before us as by magic when we take up the beautiful book which embodies and expounds the young writer's very heart; they hold it between them, the one inspiring him out of the celestial past into which she had gone, the other equally inspiring him out of the celestial unknown in which she still was. This was his poem which he chanted with his heart rent asunder by exquisite past sorrow which was not all pain, and inspired by the thrill of that unknown happiness which was to come."

It was shortly after the appearance of this first book that its author took that step upon which the happiness and success of most men's lives depend. He was married at Trélon, August 16, 1836. His bride

---

* Cardinal Wiseman's article, "St. Elizabeth of Hungary," in *Dublin Review*, October, 1837.

was the daughter of Count Félix de Mérode, a distinguished Belgian Catholic and one of the noblest characters of his day. The Abbé Gerbet celebrated the nuptial Mass, and from the eloquent address delivered by him upon the occasion we will extract this passage:

"He who has disposed, with such admirable wisdom, of the little details of the material world, to make them more in harmony with the wants of man, has provided with a care still more marvellous for the order of the spiritual world. The saints who have seen the farthest into the designs of God have thought that He has established between the souls whom He has placed on this earth secret harmonies which cause them to seek, to be attracted to, to be called reciprocally by each other when they are to tread together the ways of life and assist each other by mutual support. Those who are destined to live in retirement, far from the regard of the world, are likewise not isolated; they find there companions of their prayers and their sacrifices, prepared by God for them. It is not less certain that among those who are called to sacred marriage, among these innumerable souls, there is not one for whom God has not, from all eternity, predestined another soul who ought to be its companion, its guide, its terrestrial angel. When searching with an upright and a pure will every soul should encounter that other reserved by God, whether it is to separate from the world or to remain in it. . . ."

"I do not know," says Foisset, "but it seems difficult to despise a religion which inspires such sentiments and such thoughts."

Departing from Trélon, the happy pair journeyed

through Switzerland to Italy. In November they were in Venice; in December they arrived in Rome, where they met Lacordaire. Montalembert and his countess were accorded a triple audience by the pope, Gregory XVI., and he has given a minute account of these interviews, which we will translate for the reader:

"I presented myself at the Vatican. Scarcely had I arrived when I was ushered before the Holy Father. I kissed his sacred feet. He assisted me to rise, took my hand, holding it a long time clasped in his own and pressed against his heart, with a goodness so touching, so paternal, that I was moved to tears. He spoke to me with the greatest affection, calling me ever '*caro, carissimo conte di Montalembert.*' He congratulated me upon my attachment to the Holy See, and said, with a tone the most paternal, that it was very natural that a young man full of ardor (and he added, *of talent*) should be drawn away by the Abbé de Lamennais, but that he trusted in me as a devoted and faithful son. I was so touched, so penetrated by feelings of respect and gratitude, that I dared scarcely to speak. He congratulated himself at the proofs of detachment from Lamennais given by Lacordaire, Cambelot, and myself. I spoke of the Abbé Gerbet; he received the name rather coldly. He delivered a great eulogium on France, the king, and the French in general. He spoke to me of our bishops, of the bishop of Mans (Bouvier), of Versailles (Blanquart-Bailleul), whom he called *un santo*. In fine, after the most familiar and affectionate conversation he bade me good-by, adding, '*Au revoir!*'"

At the second audience Madame de Montalembert was present. "We were received by the pope," continues the same narrator, "in the library of the Vatican. The Holy Father treated us with the greatest cordiality, obliged us to be seated, requested us to approach nearer with our chairs, and then began to converse with us in the most animated manner. He gave us a full and detailed account of the Lamennais affair, such as it presented itself to and was treated by him. He pointed out, with good right assuredly, the extreme moderation which he had employed. He assured us that he had caused to be examined with the most scrupulous care the memorial which we had addressed him (together with other papers) by a congregation of cardinals and theologians, on whom he had imposed the pontifical secrecy, so that nothing was known of this. He expressed himself in severe terms as to the plots against his authority and the consideration due him formed by Lamennais, *e di quello da che dimorava* (Père Ventura)—'plots of which he knew very well,' said he. His praise of Lacordaire was beautiful, and he repeated to me the amiable and paternal words of the first audience. . . ."

"On the 12th of February we, Madame de Montalembert and myself, had our farewell audience with the pope. I commenced by offering him *L'Université Catholique*, wherein was to be found the admirable refutation of *Affaires de Rome* by the Abbé Gerbet. I profited by the occasion to draw the conversation to the analogous composition by Lacordaire (*Letter on the Holy See*) which the archbishop of Paris had forbidden to appear. The pope enumerated some of the insufficient reasons of M. de Quélen, as if to excuse him. I did not hesitate to say to him: 'Holy Father, there are other reasons—the political antipathies of the prelate.' The pope replied, with entire sincerity : 'I sincerely deplore the intervention of the archbishop in politics. The clergy should not mix in politics. It is not my fault if the archbishop so conducts himself. The king knows, the ambassador knows, and you know also that I have done all depending upon me to reconcile him to the government. The church is the friend of all governments, whatever be their form, provided they take not away her liberty. I am well content with Louis Philippe ; I wish all the kings of Europe resembled him. . . .'"

Of the foregoing interviews we have given all that we deemed of interest to the reader and in keeping with the subject in hand.

Part Second.

"*On ne me trouvera jamais dans les rangs de ceux qui ne défendent les bonnes causes que quand elles ne sont pas menacées, et qui les abandonnent quand elles sont sérieusement compromises, qui diminuent par conséquent leur courage et leur dévoument à mesure que le danger augmente.*"

MONTALEMBERT,
Discours 12 Juin, 1845.

PART II.

1835–1857.

I.

MONTALEMBERT took his seat in the House of Peers in 1835. By the rules governing that body he was entitled to a seat on attaining his twenty-fifth year, but could have no determining voice in its deliberations until he was thirty. He could not vote, but he might take part in its debates; and of this privilege he availed himself. He did not speak frequently nor, as a rule, at great length; but he brought to the dull discussions of the Upper House the fire of a youthful genius inspired by the loftiest principles. Those efforts embraced within this period of parliamentary abeyance, in which the youthful orator gives evidence of a studious consideration of his subject, are marked by a clearness, a comprehensiveness of political vision, a patriotic and philanthropic motive of action, and a grace and elegance of diction which would have done honor to the oldest peer who listened to their delivery. In his utterances he was ever independent, but without losing that modesty which is the greatest ornament youthful talents can possess. He was ever warm in the advocacy of his principles, unpitying to the object of his attack, without being betrayed into loss of temper or arrogance of attitude. His indignation at the oppressions of Poland and the shameful piecemealing of

Belgium endeared him to his hearers as a man having the welfare of his kind at heart ; and they admired the intelligence which scorned any lower standard in political action than the universal principles of justice. They saw in his attitude towards the government—now one of support, now one of dignified censure—an absence of all systematic attack, and the presence of that uprightness of character which, for the sake of being right, did not fear to be out of office. Finally, in the frankness, the fearlessness with which he never quailed from defending before an unsympathetic auditory, and in defiance of an infidel and intolerant press, the tenets of his faith and the aspersed hierarchy of that faith, they could not but recognize a man who loved truth for its own sake and would, if occasion offered itself, become its brilliant and formidable champion.

Notwithstanding that he had been heard upon many occasions with flattering attention by the Peers, Montalembert found himself in his thirty-second year in a position of almost complete isolation upon the two questions—freedom of the Church and freedom of education—which, through his gallant leadership, were to fuse the talents of Catholic France into a concordant body. These causes were to engross his time and his talents very largely down to 1850. The educational laws of France under the Louis Philippe régime were of a most deplorable character. The university—as the system was called—was a government monopoly of large and powerful patronage, which precluded the existence of any parallel institution. In other words, all the schools were public-schools, in the most aggravated sense with which experience under our own eyes in America enables us to endue that phrase. It alone possessed the power of teaching everything but the most elemental branches, and the so-called "right" to teach these was a *licensed* right under this system. It alone could confer the baccalaureate degree, which was, by virtue of existing laws, the *sine quâ non* to all political and professional preferment. This state of affairs forced the Catholic, *nolens volens*, to send his children to the government institutions. The reverenced representatives of his faith, the learned Jesuits and Dominicans, with whom his heart yearned to entrust his children, were banished from the sphere of education, and he was obliged either to see his children grow up in ignorance or be exposed in government schools to the loss of their faith and the ruin of their morals. These schools were maintained by the joint taxes of Catholics and unbelievers. And as the Catholics were in the majority, upon them weighed heaviest the burden of their maintenance.

As we have seen, the editors of the *Avenir* had attacked this system with vigor in 1831; and Montalembert's first utterance in the Chamber of Peers was against it. But the noise of this first onset had died away, and nothing of a thorough and organized character was done towards fomenting public opinion upon the subject until the year 1842. It is true that Montalembert in the tribune, from 1835 to 1842, had not allowed an opportunity to escape for attacking the exclusive character of the university system. But, after twelve years of broken promises on the part of the government and all too patient deferred hope upon the part of Catholics, the contest opened.

Montalembert on the 6th of June, 1842, in a speech

of admirable temper and unescapable logic, exposed the
tyranny of the educational laws. This speech was the
alarm of battle to the Catholics of France. To the existence of these schools for those who wished to send
their children there Montalembert made no objection ;
but to forcing Catholic youth there he did most strenu-
ously object as a violation of the most sacred rights of
conscience—a measure opposed to the most elemental
principles of liberty. But his opponents, unwilling to
accept his clearly-defined and logical position, pretended to see therein an attempt to overthrow the university
and substitute the clergy in its place ; and the usual
string of trite horrors which Protestant and infidel
imaginations conjure up upon such occasions was now
paraded from the tribunes of both chambers.

At the very opening of the contest, when Montalembert was preparing to deploy therein all his forces, the
failing health of his countess obliged him to accompany
her to Madeira. In the meantime the Catholic body
were not idle. The contest between the advocates of
educational freedom and the defenders of the university
continued to develop itself during the year 1843, but
outside of Parliament. Sixty bishops of France in the
meantime had uttered their dignified and determined
protest against the laws. However,

"Cœlum non animum mutant qui trans mare currunt."

From Madeira, in the fall of 1843, Montalembert sent
out his remarkable political manifesto, *Devoir des Catholiques dans la question de la liberté d'enseignement* (" Duty
of Catholics in the Question of Educational Freedom ").
Its effect was wide-spread. It moved all Catholic hearts

and marked an epoch. But to make effectual the convictions which it warmed needed action, and concerted action. Montalembert, however, was not a dreamer, a broacher of principles and theories; he was pre-eminently a man of action. In March, 1844, he hastened to France to take advantage of what had been gained and to thwart the opposition which, even among Catholics, had been shown to the decisive step—the formation of a committee to direct the disseminated forces of the Catholic body. The Archbishop of Paris was opposed to *any* committee. M. de Vatimesnil was in favor only of a *secrete* committee. Montalembert, seconded by Père de Ravignan, insisted upon an open committee, of action as well as of consultation. Pious prelates, among others the archbishop of Rouen, thought it was not a matter at all for secular interference and defence. But the favorable attitude of the papal nuncio (Mgr. Fornari) and the published utterances of the bishop of Langres to Montalembert encouraged and finally enabled him to prevail. The Electoral Committee for Religious Liberty was then constituted under the presidency of Montalembert and the vice-presidency of Vatimesnil, a former Minister of Public Instruction, and Charles Lenormant, member of the Institute. The eloquent Abbé Dupanloup and Mgr. Clausal de Montals became the advocates of the measure. "The Catholic youth were full of ardor. The incentives came directly from the pulpit of Notre Dame, just occupied, with incomparable *éclat*, during Lent by Père Ravignan, during Advent by Père Lacordaire."*

On April 15, 1844, Montalembert ascended the tri-

* Foisset.

bune in flagellation of M. Dupin's attack in the Lower House on the attitude of the clergy in regard to the university. Dupin, in his much-applauded attack, had ended with the cry, heard frequently before and since from French deputies inculcating religious intolerance: *Soyez implacables!* Montalembert's reply was a defence of the Church. However much we may admire in this speech the brilliant impetuosity of the orator, this is not the principal object of admiration which it presents. What we must most admire is the fearlessness of his attitude and the utter absence of all human considerations in his defence of the truth in the midst of a body hostile to him and his cause. These are what constitute the admirable and the heroic in his position. He stood alone, his eye flashing conviction and defiance, among the deists and materialists who surrounded him, strong in the same spirit which had sustained Paul before the Acropolis. This speech rang like a bugle-note from one end of France to the other, endearing the name of Montalembert as the champion of the faith among that people so generous and prompt in their recognition and appreciation of great abilities, especially when enlisted upon the side of the weak and the unpopular. The people of Lyons, in the ardor of their admiration, struck a bronze medal for Montalembert as the defender of the liberties of the Church, and had engraved upon it the famous words with which this speech closed : " We are the sons of Crusaders, and we will not recoil before the sons of Voltaire." Seven days later, April 23, the debate opened upon the new *projet de loi* introduced by Villemain, Minister of Public Instruction. The effect of this project, if it became a law, would only

be to strengthen the university in its monopoly an[d]
hamper with destructive requirements the non-govern[mental]
mental elementary schools. Its supporters came, re[-]
cruited from the arsenals of hatred and sophistry, to i[ts]
defence. Montalembert met them at every point an[d]
refuted them—upon the grounds of history, of politic[al]
ethics, and of contemporary experience. Of the la[w]
under discussion he said :

"It substitutes for a *statu quo* which is detestable [a]
future even more alarming. Not only does it maintai[n]
the university, with its fiscal and inquisitory spirit, a[nd]
the custom-house of intelligence, but by exigencies un[-]
heard of before . . . it will within a brief period de[-]
stroy all the private institutions now in existence.

. . . .

"I do not know whence comes this dangerous foll[y]
of modern states, and especially of a certain school i[n]
France who wish to impose upon governments the rôl[e]
of doing everything, of conducting, of absorbing ever[y]
thing. 'The smaller the number of things over which
government exercises its authority, the longer shall th[e]
government last.' 'Tis not I who have said this ; 't[is]
not the utterance of a Jesuit nor an Ultramontane ; the[y]
are the words of Aristotle, and I conclude from the[m]
that you who wish to extend your authority over th[at]
which heretofore has been respected—that you will n[ot]
last very long.

"Never, even in the most absolute states, since Chri[s-]
tianity has transformed the world, has any one eve[r]
dreamed until our day of this direct and exclusive i[n-]
tervention of the state in education. This destructi[ve]
doctrine has its foundation in the past only upon th[e]

authority of Minos, of Lycurgus, and of Robespierre—that is to say, it is founded upon fable, upon paganism, and upon that which is worse than paganism. . . .

. . . .

"To resume: You are in presence of two systems—the system of despotism and the system of liberty; and to personify them I will call them the English system and the Russian system.

"The English system, where, alongside of venerable and fecund institutions especially adopted by the state and sanctioned by religion, there is complete liberty for others. The Russian system, where the iron hand of power has invaded even the education of the hearth, and where no one can even be a preceptor without ministerial sanction.

"Evidently your law tends twenty times more to the Russian than to the English side—more to the side of barbarity organized by despotism than to the side of civilization enriched by political dignity and independence. . . ."

Such is the tone of this strong discourse. Fain would we reproduce in their entirety its bursts of indignant sarcasm, its resistless onset of eloquent argument, its graceful transitions to the facetious and the amiable. But we have not the space to follow the orator in his course demonstrating the sceptical fruitfulness of the university system—its injustice to Catholic parents; its maintenance against the earnest protests of sixty bishops voicing the sentiments of millions of their flocks; its violation of all political canons, as shown by the writings and speeches of numerous authorities.

The debate was carried on by Montalembert and his colleagues, Baron Séguier, the Marquis de Barthélemy, and Count Beugnot, from April 6 to May 21, during which period he made, besides the discourse just quoted from and those passages-at-arms which are the accompaniment of every debate, two set speeches full of splendid thought and powerful argument. His discourse delivered upon the 8th of May in defence of the religious orders excluded from teaching even elementary branches contains a review of the history of monasticism and a defence and review of the history of the Jesuits, and is a masterpiece of historical summary. Considering the proscriptive effects of the bill, the orator stops a moment to pay a tribute to the Jesuit and Dominican—Ravignan and Lacordaire—who were then filling France with the wonders of their eloquence, and to point out the merciless injustice of a law destined to exclude such men from even the most elemental branches of instruction.

The habile and unprincipled Left and their organs, and those of the Right in sympathy with them, feeling their walls of defence crumbling under the strokes of their opponents, did that, says Montalembert, which men do in a place besieged. They made a cunning diversion—a vigorous sortie. They were attacked in the name of liberty and the Church, and they could not withstand. They made a detour. They fell upon the most vulnerable flank of their opponents: they raised a cry against the Jesuits. Thiers, who was one of those who study that they may follow to their advantage the tides and currents of popular prejudice, in compliance with the clamors of the Left began his attack upon the

Jesuits in 1845, and the timorous ministry followed in the wake.*

In no utterances was Montalembert more eloquent, more terrible to withstand, than when he arraigned before the house and the country that ministry in its shameful subserviency to an opposition "which in its demands gave the lie to all its professed principles, which had ascended the course of the ages and rummaged the bowels of the past, to draw forth therefrom proscription and servitude to impose them upon their fellow-citizens."†

Where prejudice has warped the reason arguments are of little avail. The odious measure was voted by the Chamber of Peers. But although the government seemed to triumph with its ready majorities, the Catholic cause was only more firmly welded by the blow. The government was alarmed by the feelings among the Catholic body, and, by an inconsequence natural to injustice, pointed to Montalembert, who was the Achilles of the Catholic cause, as the originator of the discontent. As if, indeed, the opposer and not the proposer of evil laws was to be held responsible for their effects!

---

* Alison (*History of Europe*), in his account of the educational question, has done nothing more than follow Thiers and inaptly quote Montalembert. He has gone into the hypothecation of motives; the facts he has ignored. He quotes Thiers' statement that the clergy were conspiring to overthrow the university. He does not quote Montalembert where he demands that same freedom in education which England enjoyed; and, as if the *locus quo* could control the principles of liberty, Alison becomes the champion of a state of things in France which he would scorn to advocate for Great Britain, or would be scorned and hooted did he advocate them there. He has wofully missed the whole issue either through lack of diligence in his research or through preponderance of prejudice in his judgment. But as we are not as venturesome as Alison in divining motives, we will not decide which.

† Speech on the measure announced against the Jesuits, June 11, 1845—*Discours*, vol. ii. p. 173.

By the Catholics Montalembert was recognized as the champion of violated consciences, and addresses and letters in praise of his efforts came from all quarters, assuring him of the admiration of the good and the great, "which, after the testimony of conscience to a sacred duty worthily accomplished, is the sweetest recompense a noble heart can receive."

The bill was sent to the Lower House, where it remained unacted upon when the Chamber of Deputies was dissolved in June, 1846. So that the efforts of Montalembert were not wholly without fruit. In his pamphlet, *The Duty of Catholics in the Approaching Elections*, he thus summarizes the political history of the last three years: "We had against us all that was popular, influential, and powerful—a large majority in both chambers, ninety-nine out of every hundred of the newspapers; we have had against us the tribunals and the academies, the Council of State and the College of France, the intrigues of diplomats in Rome and the pride of false science in Paris, statesmen and thinkers, sophists and legists. And yet we have not been conquered!"

This pamphlet bore fruit, and the next chamber saw a number of eminent Catholics among its number. *One hundred and twenty-two* deputies had pledged themselves to protect the Catholic interests.

Salvandy, new Minister of Public Instruction, withdrew in consequence the Villemain educational project and announced one of his own fabrication, suggesting some mitigation of the rigors of the former law, but by no means granting the educational freedom demanded. This new bill was never debated. Montalembert attacked it, however, in the columns of the *Correspondant*, and " literally pulverized it," says Foisset. But the country was laboring in the throes of an approaching crisis, and more violent elements than those of Catholic agitation, which confined itself within constitutional bourns, were demanding the attention of the government.

II.

Early in 1848 Montalembert uttered his famous speech on the "Sonderbund." Seven Catholic and conservative cantons of Switzerland had formed a defensive league to resist the attacks of radicals against the ancient federal constitution of the country. The Diet, under the control of the radical elements, pronounced the dissolution of the "Sonderbund." The seven cantons protested through their deputies. The thirteen radical cantons answered by sending an army against them. The seven cantons yielded one after another upon conditions which the majority broke as soon as the minority were in their power. The most shameful confiscation was established; the provisional government passed *ex post facto* laws to aid them in their violence; the ministers of religion, Catholic and Protestant, were shorn of their rights; even the Sisters of Charity were driven like cattle, with three days' notice, from the country; nothing was too sacred to escape the avarice and the fury of these unbridled factions. The French government by prompt interference could have prevented these horrors and desecrations; but, in the characteristic lethargy of its foreign policy, did nothing.

". . . What was at stake at the other side of the Jura were not the Jesuits nor the cantonal sovereignty; it was European order and peace, the security of the world and of France; that is what has been vanquished, stifled, crushed at our gates, upon our frontiers, by men who would ask nothing less than to launch from **our side** of the Alps and the Jura the brands **of** discord, **of war,** and of anarchy. (*Très-bien! très-bien!*) Therefore I do not come to speak in behalf of the vanquished, but to the vanquished—vanquished myself to those who have been vanquished; that is, to the representatives of the social order, of the liberal order, of the social regularity which has been vanquished in Switzerland, and which are menaced in all Europe by a new invasion of the barbarians. (*Sensation*.) . . .

"Last year the last vestige of Polish nationality was wiped out; this year the first cradle of European liberty is a victim to a similar attempt. Only last year the crime was that of absolute monarchies; this year it is committed by pretended liberals who are at heart tyrants of the very worst species. But then as to-day what have we witnessed? The abuse of force, the stifling of liberty, of right, by a brutal and impious violence (*nombreuses marques d'approbation*); the violation of sworn faith, the superiority of number erected into a dogma, and falsehood serving as the arm and apparel of violence. (*Nouvelles marques d'approbation*.)

. . . .

"Let no one come here to say, as certain blind but generous spirits have, that radicalism is the exaggeration of liberalism. No, it is its antipode, it is its extreme opposite; radicalism is nothing else than the exaggeration of despotism (*très-bien! très-bien!*), and never did despotism assume a form more odious. Liberty is rational and voluntary tolerance; radicalism is absolute intolerance which stops only before the impossible. Liberty imposes upon no one useless sacrifices; radicalism submits not to a thought, a word, a prayer opposed to its will. Liberty sanctifies the rights of minorities; radicalism absorbs and destroys them. In a word, liberty is respect for man, while radicalism is the hatred of man raised to its greatest intensity. (*Vive approbation.*) No, never did Muscovite despot, never did tyrant of the Orient, more despise his kind than these radical clubbists who gag their vanquished adversaries in the name of liberty and equality. (*Très-bien!*)

"I believe, moreover, that no one has a better right to proclaim this distinction, for I challenge any one to love liberty more than myself. And here I must remark that I wish to accept neither as a reproach nor as a eulogium that which the Minister of Foreign Affairs said to me recently, that I was exclusively devoted to religious liberty. No, no, gentlemen, that to which I have been devoted is liberty in its entirety, liberty for all and in all things. I have always defended, always proclaimed it. I, who have written so much, said so much —far too much, I acknowledge (*non! non!*)—I defy any one to find a word emanating from my pen or fallen from my lips which was not destined to serve liberty. Liberty!—ah! I can say it without circumlocution, it has been the idol of my soul (*mouvement*); if I have any reproach to make myself it is that I have loved it too well, loved as one loves when young—that is to say, without measure, without stint. But I do not reproach myself, I do not regret it; I wish to continue to serve it, to love it always, to believe in it always! (*Très-bien!*) And I believe that I have never loved it more nor served it better than on that day when I have forced myself to tear off the mask of its enemies, who garb themselves in its colors, who usurp its flag to soil and to dishonor it. (*Marques unanimes et prolongées d'assentiment.*) . . ."

The orator ceased amid prolonged bursts of applause. The sitting was suspended. The peers quit their seats under the influence of the discourse and formed in the hemicycle in numerous and animated groups. Guizot, President of the Council and Minister of Foreign Affairs, notwithstanding Montalembert's censure of the government, refused to mar the effect of the speech by a reply. In the fervor of their admiration many peers forgot the rules of the House and demanded that the speech be printed.

This was his last speech before the Chamber of Peers. It was the brilliant sunset of the first part of his public career, giving promise of a brighter to-morrow. Six weeks later the elements so mercilessly condemned in that speech overthrew the government and added it to the rubbish of revolution.

III.

With the monarchy of Louis Philippe disappeared Montalembert's, and with it all other peerages; in its stead came the Republic of 1848. For a time a cloud of dismal foreboding rested upon him, and a recurrence of the horrors of '93 seemed not improbable. But power fell partly into the hands of men who swayed the clubs. Their influence held the *émeutiers* at bay till the better elements of society, being reassured by the absence of any very extravagant outbreaks, took courage and rallied around Lamartine, who was then enjoying the high tide of a popularity which had been obtained by a skilful middle course during the previous months and by means of his *Girondins*, in which book he had "poetized the most shameful features of the Revolution." * After the first shock Montalembert, accepting the situation with as much grace as his fears admitted of, proceeded to extend and systematize the action of the Catholic body through France in behalf of public order and settled government. The series of political manifestoes issued by him during the first year of the Republic, as president of the "Electoral Committee of Religious Freedom," are masterpieces of political wisdom and of the highest literary excellence. Many departments desired him for their representative. He was elected from the department of Doubs.

Radicalism, socialism, and red-republicanism were now rife in Paris, Lyons, and Marseilles. Every day the action of the clubs became more alarming, and, until their entire suppression by Napoleon as emperor, they continued for four years to keep the country in a ferment. These three cities were the repeated theatres

---

* It is seldom that the pen and the voice of a deputy have ever become so potent with the mass, who make and unmake dynasties, as Lamartine's had. Sage judges have not hesitated to give his pen and voice the unenviable praise of having by their power precipitated the Revolution of 1848. See N. Wm. Senior's *Journal*, 1848-1852, Conversations with Alphonse de Tocqueville etc. vol. i.

of the insurrections and murders which those elements, led by bad and ambitious men—Blanc, Ledru-Rollin, Albert, Blanqui, Proudhon—continued to incite. Montalembert, seeing in this complexion of affairs the ruin of the whole social fabric, pledged himself to his constituents to meet these elements with a most vigorous opposition. "I will combat not only Communism properly so-called, which dares not show itself in all its revoltful nudity, but that Communism, still more dangerous, which presents itself under the form of fiscal laws, excessive imposts, forced appropriations, new monopolies; which tends throughout to substitute the state for the individual, to gather gradually all of the products and all of the forces of the country into the hands of power, and which, could it triumph, would dry up all the sources of industry, of art, of intelligence, of spontaneous effort, would carry disorder and misery beneath the most humble roofs, and would make France, impoverished and enslaved, the laughing-stock of Europe." This was the political chart which guided him until he left public life.

The worst apprehensions were realized by the terrific insurrection of Red Republicans and Communists in June following in the streets of Paris, which lasted seventy hours and cost France more generals than the battle of Beresina or the field of Waterloo.

Montalembert supported Louis Napoleon's candidacy for president, being convinced by the attitude of Cavaignac that France would in two years of his régime be ruined morally and materially. He was the first man of eminence who announced his support, but others soon followed his example—Barrot, Thiers, Berryer, Molé. It was, after all, but a question of alternatives.

IV.

The period of the Republic has been pronounced, by a critic * whose praise will not be suspected, the golden period of Montalembert's career. And it is so, not because religious and educational freedom, which had been to a certain extent the cause of his life so far, in exclusion of general politics, was not one worthy the devotion of the highest abilities; but it was so because this cause broadened out under the Republic into the domain of the vast and imperative wants of a society racked to its centre. The cause of educational and religious liberty was now not alone at stake; but those sister-principles, equally great and equally elemental, which lie at the base of human society and are its sustaining force were also involved. The formidable advocate of a single measure, to which he has marshalled the efforts of a life, may cease to be great when the line of defence and attack stretches out to embrace the universal principles of government. It was because in this new field he displayed not only all of his old prowess, but even surpassed his former efforts, that he has, as well as others, considered this the brightest period of his public service. It was under the Republic that all his former efforts were to bear fruit and the rectitude of their aim to be admitted, and even applauded, by those who had hitherto been his implacable opponents.

Coming from the sedate Chamber of Peers, where

* Sainte-Beuve.

nothing but a faint **and** occasional expression **of coun**-ter-sentiment interrupted the orator in the impetuosity of utterance seeking the expression **of** swifter thought, he found himself, in the assemblies **of** the Republic, stopped in almost every period by *rumeurs et dénégations, bruits, exclamations, rires, tumultes* from **the** Left; like a fiery steed accustomed to a free rein, **who** falls **to** the possession of a master who **at** every manifestation of metal seeks by a rude and unreasonable **use of the** curb to break his courage and subdue his pride. But sustained by his **own** fearlessness and encouraged by the applause of the majority **of the** house—the representatives of **the** peaceful elements of society—he **did not** succumb **to the** clamors **of** empirics **and** anarchists. Ay, more, he taught **them to** cower **under** his glance **and** crouch **beneath the lash of** wholesome **truths** forcibly expressed.*

* " **Up to** this time he was admired, **but not** followed except by those belonging to his immediate party. Now [November 5, 1849, is the date of the article] he is followed willingly by the representatives of all parties. Not only the **eloquence and** brilliancy but the meaning of his noble speeches is accepted and acknowledged " (Sainte-Beuve, *Premiers Lundis*).

" He is always perfectly at ease. He has **few** gestures, but **he** possesses the qualities essential to successful action. His voice, pure and sustained (*d'une longue haleine*), is distinct and clear, with **a** vibration and accent easily marking the generous or the ironical. The son of an English mother, he has in his voice, through its sweetness, a certain rise and fall of accentuation which answers his purpose well, letting certain words drop from a greater height and resound further than others. I ask pardon for these particulars; but the ancients, our masters in everything, particularly in eloquence, gave a minute attention to them, and a great modern orator has said, ' A man has always the voice of his mind ' " (*Ib.*).

Another description of his person may be grateful to the reader. 'Tis by the Abbé Dourlens:

" His action is the external manifestation of this eloquence. His gestures are sober, but easy, noble, dignified, aristocratic. His head slightly thrown back gives him an aspect of provocation (*ton provocateur*). A perpetual smile trembles upon his lips, and, changing from moment to moment, becomes by turns benevolent, disdainful, and satirical. His eyes, which are large and melancholy, show in succession with glances of energy all the different sentiments expressed."

It was not till the 22d of June, four months after the revolution, that he raised his voice in the Constituent Assembly. It was to combat a measure of the Provisional Government for the forced purchase by the state of all the railroad lines in France.

". . . I find in this project," he said, "an attack upon the right of property, which is the base of all society—an attack upon the spirit of association, which, it seems to me, is a peculiar property of democracy and the sole guarantee of its advantages. . . .

"The Minister of Finance has said that the spirit of association applied to public works can only co-exist with monarchical and aristocratic institutions. This opinion is refuted by the opinions of the liberal philosophers whom I have just quoted; again, by the example of Russia—that is to say, the most absolute monarchy in existence, and which, on the contrary, has precisely applied to public works that very principle of which you demand the triumph in the name of democracy. . . .

"Let us not assert that which I am contending for is an English or an American principle; let us say, what is the truth, that it is a liberal principle. Let us recognize that the contest is not between aristocracy or royalty on the one side and democracy on the other; the contest is between the spirit of liberty and the spirit of monopoly, between exaggerated centralization and the free development of individual forces, the free development of the principle of association."

The result of this project, had it become a law, would have been to increase by a frightful numerical accession the army of bureaucrats. But in this measure the socialist, who is at heart the most aggravated of egotists, saw a new realm open to his plunder, just as the **Communist Courber, the leader of** the ruffians who razed the *Colonne Vendôme,* avowed that personal **avarice and** not political conviction **had** dictated him. The metal it contained **was what** he coveted. This measure would, moreover, have propagated **a spirit of distrust and unrest** fatal to all extended industry, **and thrown down at once** the barriers against **irrational** legislation, **whose** tendency is **ever** towards establishing **the communism of the state** upon **the** ruins **of** individual and corporate **industries. In these** matters, **said** Montalembert, "**il n'y a** que **le premier** pas qui coûte."

This **discourse is a masterful congeries of all the** principles **which should guide a state that, having** entered upon **the turbulent sea of democracy, finds itself** confronted **with difficulties of this character. Its** value **cannot change until the present trend of the** world **towards** universal democracy **has also changed.** Throughout **its** delivery **the majority of the house** encouraged him **by** vehement **applause, and when he** ceased **large numbers crowded around to cover him with their congratulations.**

In the same spirit he advocated with **all his power** the necessity **of** constituting **two legislative chambers.** Only a summary **of this speech** remains. **He advocated, too, the dissolution of the** Constituent Assembly on **the** ground **that it was not in sympathy with** the **new** president **of the Republic, harmony between executive and** legislative **departments being of great importance in** the present juncture. **This speech was** delivered amid the most shameful **interruptions** from the **Left.**

But it was the expression of the sentiments of the majority. The measure was carried.

These speeches gave him at once a prominent position in the Conservative ranks. Mr. Senior, the friend of Alexis de Tocqueville, who was in Paris, says in his *Journal:* "Molé, Thiers, Montalembert, Broglie, and Berryer are considered the heads of the coalition which calls itself the party of order, or the moderate party. . . . They have been nicknamed the five Burgraves." *

Animosities outside of the Radical ranks, which had sprung mostly from conflicting interests, ceased almost wholly during the first years of the Republic. A common danger had made a common cause, and men stood together who had stood opposed for decades. "It was a time when the bad had combined, and the good felt the necessity of associating together, or else fall, one by one, an unpitied sacrifice in a contemptible struggle."

To the minds of a large number of the Constituent Assembly there seemed nothing too sacred to entitle it to escape the rude touch of innovation. Among other radical measures it was proposed to reconstitute the judiciary. Montalembert offered an amendment tending to give to the principle of irremovability (*quamdiu se bene gesserint*), proclaimed in theory by the constitution, a practical and immediate guarantee. That it was an occasion where arguments of the strongest character were demanded, and the presentation of the principle involved in the amendment in the most convincing manner was necessary, is evident from the fact that the vote in favor of Montalembert's proposition had a majority of but twenty voices.

* *Journals kept in France and Italy,* 1848 *to* 1852.

V.

The Constituent Assembly dissolved, Montalembert was one of an electoral committee charged with looking after the interests of the Conservative party—a fusion of Orleanists, Legitimists, and Republicans—as opposed to the reactionists in the elections of 1848. He was re-elected by his former constituents, and was also returned by the department of Côtes-du-Nord.

When Rossi, the pope's minister, was assassinated, and the day following Monsignore Palma, the pope's secretary, shot down by his side, and Pius IX. himself was obliged to escape from Rome in disgrace before men of the same principles who had overthrown the Swiss cantons and raised the red flag in the streets of Paris, General Cavaignac, then dictator in France, sent to the pope's assistance thirty-five hundred men. The following year, when, regaining possession of his estates, he was entering Rome, Napoleon informed the pope, through Colonel Ney, the conditions upon which he was to resume his authority, in terms* as uncalled for as they were insulting to all the past liberal measures of the pope—measures which had been used by the revolutionists only as a means to terrorize and anarchize.

The commission charged with an examination of the credits relative to the expedition to Rome pronounced itself energetically in favor of the absolute indepen-

* "Amnistie générale, secularisation des emplois, promulgation à Rome du Code Napoléon." This was simply a piece of electoral claptrap used by Napoleon and meant to count with the masses in France, whom he was secretly and systematically winning over to his favor preparatory to the *coup-d'état* and the re-establishment of the Empire.

dence of the Sovereign Pontiff. And Thiers (*mirabile dictu!*) was its author.

"Without the authority," he said, " of the Sovereign Pontiff Catholic unity would be dissolved ; without this unity Catholicism would perish in the midst of sects, and the moral world, already so terribly shaken, would be destroyed from centre to circumference."

Victor Hugo, amid the acclamations of the Left, on the 19th of October, 1849, took occasion to glorify this action of Napoleon and asperse the pope. To this speech Montalembert replied before its echo had died out, and before had subsided the passions of hate on the one side, and of indignation and alarm on the other, which it had aroused.

The opening words of Montalembert fell like a bursting bomb amid the Radicals who blackened the benches of the Left, always to a greater or less degree a rookery of violent passions never silent. " The speech," he said, " to which you have just listened has received the chastisement it merited in the applause with which it has been welcomed." Immediately the Assembly, beginning at the Left, was thrown into a violent tumult beggaring description, which the efforts of the president, at first impotent, at last succeeded in sufficiently quelling to allow Montalembert to utter another sentence.

"Since the word chastisement wounds you, gentlemen (addressing the Left), I withdraw it, and I substitute in its place that of *recompense*." This was followed by another series of tumults more violent, if possible, than the former, and requiring more effort and time upon the part of the president to suppress. At last, as if exhausted by their paroxysms of rage, they allowed Montalembert to continue, but with the usual *rumeurs* and *reclamations* throughout the course of the speech, in the midst or at the end of the expression of every ennobling sentiment. He first demolished the position of the Radical champion, reviewed in a rapid and masterly manner the supine results of monarchic interference with the papacy, went over the whole question of the temporal authority of the pope, painted the personal career of Pius IX., and used words of the most pathetic and stirring eloquence in speaking of the Church.

"His speech," says the *Journal des Débats*, "ended amidst storms of applause such as were unknown before to deliberative assemblies." Throughout its delivery the majority of the house were in a perfect fever of enthusiasm, and repeatedly stopped the orator to give expression to the most lively commendation—now by long cheers and bravos, again and again by triple salvos of applause. The orator's sentiments were sanctioned by the carriage of the measure in behalf of which he spoke by a vote of 467 to 168. The triumph of this speech was even greater than that of the discourse upon the "Sunderbund."

"This victory was sweet to his heart," says Madam Oliphant*—"more sweet than any simply political victory could have been. He records it in his journal with a thrill of gratified emotion." "The Right applauded with such enthusiasm," he says, "as to make their cheers resemble an act of faith. It was the finest moment of my life. . . . The attitude of the Assembly was like a solemn adhesion to the Church. One man said that his impulse had been to go at once to confession." Thiers,

* In her *Memoir of Montalembert.*

his old opponent, whose good opinion was worth having, said of him: "He is the most eloquent of men and his speech the finest I ever heard. I envy him for it, but I hope the envy is no sin; for I love the beautiful and I love Montalembert." Berryer addressed him these words: "Your strength lies in this, that you are not absolute but resolute." Sainte-Beuve, the lavish admirer of everything pagan, concedes so much to the moderns as to say that "the passage concerning the Church, that pathetic impersonation, even for those who regard it only from a distance and from an artistic point of view, must remain one of the happiest inspirations of eloquence."

Some of the passages of this speech are not only worthy of remark for their beauty but for the transition which they mark in his politics from the stand which Montalembert took, in the settled state of society under the monarchy of Louis Philippe, in favor of unlimited freedom, to the distrust, which the violent action of the Radical elements had created in his mind, of France being worthy of so large a fund of liberties. Not that he *loved* liberty any the less. But he felt that there were large and aggressive numbers who would only make an abuse of it and turn it into an engine for overturning society.

"... We have received a frightful defeat. Our experience has turned not only against us, not only against Pius IX., but against liberty herself. (*Bravos nombreux à droite.*) It is on this account that I would bring here before me all those demagogues, all those reactionists of whom I have but just spoken, and for once tell them the truth. (*Vive approbation à droite. Rumeurs à gauche.*)

"À Droite.—*Très-bien! très-bien! Parlez! parlez!*

"M. de Montalembert—Listen, then, to that truth. If I could address all of them at once I would say: Are you aware of what is the greatest of all your crimes before the world? It is not alone the blood of the innocent shed by you, although it cries to Heaven for vengeance against you; it is not alone that you have sown ruins with a lavish hand throughout Europe, although this might be the most formidable of arguments against your doctrines. No! It is that you have disenchanted the world of liberty. (*Acclamations à droite: Très-bien! très bien!*) It is that you have in some way disoriented the world! It is that you have compromised or overthrown or annihilated in all honest hearts that noble belief! It is that you have rolled back towards its source the torrent of human destinies! (*Applaudissements prolongés sur les bancs de la majorité.*)"

Owing to the incendiary, aggressive, and blasphemous state of the press of Paris and throughout the country, wherever the reactionists' principles were represented, Montalembert became one of the advocates of restraining laws. "I commenced," he said, "some fourteen years ago my political career by voting and speaking against the [press] laws of September. I come to-day to vote and to speak for a law which in my opinion is much more severe than those laws of September. But I am not the only one obliged so to act. (*Rires ironiques à gauche.*) Others more illustrious than myself are in the same position. . . ."

He then proceeds to paint the character, the conduct, and the nocent influence of that press which had abused its liberty and surpassed all limits, adding to the corrupted masses of the city a stimulant to revolt, and among the ignorant and credulous of the rural population, whom it had found pure and peaceful, cultivating an appetite which was fast making that population corrupt too by the eagerness and rapidity with which it was assimilating the food of communistic errors and misrepresentations.

Certain writers who have spoken of Montalembert's career between 1848 and 1852 have thought that they had discovered in his attitude a change of principles.* He would indeed be a strange statesman who should insist upon applying always the same remedy to every complexion of disorder. It was a change, not of principles, but simply a change of the remedy for that society which he found so very ill. Here are his own words :

"I vote for this project, certainly not because it is opposed to the liberty of the press, but because, on the contrary, it is for the liberty of the press, because it is destined to preserve us from a dictatorship, because it is destined to preserve liberty from its own excesses, to render an homage and a service to that liberty which I have always loved, always served, and wish ever to continue to serve and to love."

For the same reasons are we to account for Montalembert's being one of the most active of a commission of seventeen † who elaborated a *projet de loi* upon electoral

---

* Mrs. Oliphant's *Memoir of Montalembert*, and Sainte-Beuve.

† This commission was composed as follows : MM. Benoit d'Azy, Berryer, Beugnot, De Broglie, Buffet, De Chasseloup-Laubat, Daru, Léon Faucher, Jules de Lasteyrie, Molé, De Montalembert, De Montebello, Piscatory, De Sèze, le General de Saint-Priest, Thiers, De Vatimesnil. They constituted the eminence, the talent, and the eloquence of the National Assembly. They were, of course, a shining mark for the diatribes of the democratic press. "The heads," said the *Voix du Peuple*, " of these *vieillards entêtés* are pledged to the infernal gods of the revolution."

reform which was not an *abolition* (as false or ignorant critics have called it) of universal suffrage, but simply a limitation and regulation of universal suffrage. The law proposed was similar to laws regulating the suffrage of the United States—it required a three years' domicile before the exercise of the right of suffrage. It was aimed at the vagrant, turbulent, and irresponsible voters who, under previous laxity governing voting, were focussed upon doubtful departments where some prominent Radical was seeking an election. A law directed towards the mitigation of such abuses needs no apology.

Out of the debate on this measure resulted a very lively passage-at-arms between Montalembert and Victor Hugo, in which these antipodal champions met in the shock of single combat. The Left cheered Hugo and interrupted Montalembert; the Right applauded Montalembert and interrupted Hugo. Hugo was goaded by the interruptions, but Montalembert was not. Their strokes were terrific; but Montalembert's were too rapid, too direct, too vigorous to be withstood. Montalembert struck twice to Hugo's once. Hugo fought with denunciation; but Montalembert used sarcasm, humor, ridicule, and facts.

During the prorogation of the National Assembly in 1850 Montalembert went to Rome for rest and change. While there the municipality, with the approval of Pius IX., sent him, through their president, Prince Pierre Odescalchi, a diploma of Roman citizen with a gold medal commemorative of his voyage. This title has been but rarely conferred upon strangers. Petrarch was the first. Generals Oudinot and Rostolan, commanders of the expeditionary army, were the last to be

invested. The illustrious La Moricière had received it
after the battles of Castel Fidardo and Ancona.

VI.

The vexed question of education was to reach a solution under the Republic. On the 18th of September, 1848, Montalembert ascended the tribune of the Assemblée Constituante to urge an amendment to the constitution tending to that end. It was a field in which he was a master; and the forty-four octavo pages embracing his discourse attest by their crystallized thought the deep consideration the subject had received. At the Left the speech was met by that intolerance with which the egotists and hypocrites of the Mountain have always sought to stifle all utterance disconsonant to their own opinions. They wearied him by their interruptions, but they did not conquer him. Goaded by constant interruptions, he never lost his temper; but, on the contrary, as if to give the highest proof of balance, at times the least looked for discomfited the Left by the finest strokes of that caustic and playful humor which characterizes his eloquence. The main point of this speech was that the liberty demanded was an imprescriptible right. But we cannot go into an analysis even of its arguments. It should be read to be appreciated. The old phantoms this question had always raised, of a monopoly on the part of religious orders as the result of any concession by the state, was shown again to be baseless. He demonstrated to them that the tendency of the state system had been to recruit the ranks of socialism. From the educational halls of the state have gone forth the utopists and innovators, the venom of whose philosophy was corrupting France everywhere; not only in the centres of commerce and manufacture, but in distant cantons heretofore untainted. Though this speech failed to carry the amendment, its masterful exposé of the sources of the social evils of France bore fruit in many minds within and out of the Assembly. It dissipated much of the prejudice heretofore encumbering the discussion, and it aided the more enlightened and influential spirits who fortunately were in the majority in the next house to see the educational question in the proper light.

Soon after the opening of the new session of 1848 M. de Falloux, the new Minister of Public Instruction, busied himself to prepare a *projet de loi* which would respond at once to the wishes of the advocates of educational freedom and the exigencies of the constitution. To this end he named a commission, with Thiers as president, and composed of eleven representatives, among whom was Montalembert, three members of the old royal council of the university—one of whom was Cousin—and eight other gentlemen familiar with the question, and among these was the Abbé Dupanloup. After devoting much time and labor to the discussion and study of the subject in their chambers the commission presented on the 18th of June, 1849, a *projet* providing for the abolition of all previous authorization for opening a school and of the certificate of studies heretofore required; a radical reform in primary education; disfranchisement of the little seminaries in charge of religious, and the freedom of religious congregations heretofore interdicted from teaching ; and although extending the surveillance of the state over the little seminaries, as the constitution imperiously demanded, *limited* this surveillance to questions *of public order only.* Montalembert accepted the *projet.* The result was a breach between Louis Veuillot and himself, brought on by the violent attacks of the editor of the *Univers,* and the result, says Foisset, was "the decapitation of the **Catholic party."** It was a compromise which circumstances demanded, and results justified Montalembert's action. Louis Veuillot stigmatized it "comme une secrète **defaillance de la** raison et du cœur." But there came from a higher judge, and one whose judgment both could respect, an endorsement of Montalembert. It came as a balm to the wound which, as a man of **lofty and disinterested purpose, he must** have received in having his motives questioned by those who sat with him at the same political hearthstone. Pius IX. sent a special despatch through his nuncio expressing his entire satisfaction with his conduct and that of MM. les Comtes Molé and De Falloux. But Montalembert **never regained after** this breach that wide-spread influence which he before possessed over the Catholic body. Such is the power of the leaders of the press, their influence **for good or for evil.** The **hasty** and unconsidered **calumny is sent out.** But no denial can ever overtake **all the evil it sets afoot.** *Vox missa nescit reverti.*

. The most astonishing feature of the history of this **treaty, as** Montalembert **called it,** is that, while it is practically a complete **victory for his** cause (since the surveillance **reserved** to the university was disciplinary only), Adolphe Thiers was the president of the committee presenting and approving the *projet*, and Cousin one of its advocates. These bitter antagonists of religious and educational **freedom** under the monarchy—Thiers, **in the** Lower House, scourging **the Jesuits** and conjuring **religious** phantoms ; Cousin, in **the Chamber of** Peers, fighting Montalembert, with weapons from the same **arsenal**, at every step—range themselves alongside of the **son of** the Crusaders and become the upholders **of his** long-fought-for cause. **One** feels tempted to ask, **if the peaceful demands** of **the Catholics** of France were a **menace and** a danger, as proclaimed, under Louis Philippe's régime, **how** is it **that,** when society was shaken **to** its foundations and fear dwelt **in** all hearts, Thiers and Cousin could recommend those very reforms which **were** so terrible before to their sensitive **imaginations ?**

Thiers had to **and did confess : "I say it frankly, the** partisans **of the** Church, **the partisans** of the state, are for **me the** defenders **of** society, of that **society,** which I believe to be **in** peril, and **I have** given them my hand. I have given it **to** M. de Montalembert ; I still **hold out** my hand **to** him, and I hope that, in spite **of our different** points of **view, it shall** remain **in his** for the common defence **of** society. . . . "

But this was **not all ; there** is still another feature of this victory **not less** humiliating to Thiers. Before the final passage **of the educational** bill an amendment was proposed against **the Jesuits. Who was its** most memorable opponent ? That very Adolphe Thiers "in a memorable discourse," says Montalembert, "when he proved that the constitution, in promising liberty to all, interdicted **every** repressive measure against the Jesuits." The proposed amendment was rejected by 450 against 148 voices.

VII.

After the vacation of 1851 it became evident that another political crisis was approaching. The next year the present Assembly would reach the term of its existence and the president of the Republic would be retired, being re-eligible under the constitution. The Duke de Broglie proposed that the constitution be amended in order to make the president eligible for a second term. Montalembert supported this proposition, believing that, under the circumstances, it was the only proper course. But the project failed. A large number of those who had heretofore constituted the Conservative majority of the house divided off, some coalescing with the Left, some ranging themselves under the standard of Legitimacy. All party men poised themselves for a change, all standing ready, for the sake of their own success, to coalesce with the partisans of any other régime.

Montalembert thought he saw in the new attitude of parties a condition of things which might result in another dictator. Thiers foresaw autocracy. "*L'Empire c'est fait*," he said June 18, 1851. As Montalembert had no predilections, was not a party man, he supported Napoleon as the representative of order and authority. He was in reality deceived by the modest demeanor and calm utterances of the prince-president. But he was not alone in his illusion. Under the empire of this illusion he made his speech of February 10, 1851, in favor of the president. It not only displeased Napoleon by its reservations, but it estranged from Montalembert all the chiefs of the majority. Again the victim of independent and conscientious action, he found himself in a position of political isolation.

The state of affairs induced by the opposition between executive and legislative branches led to the *coup-d'état* of December 2, 1851, whereby, with the army at his back, Napoleon took into his hands all the reins of government. The change came as silently as snow that falls in the night. Astonished Paris awakened the next morning, and in the placards which covered the walls read this last feature of her checkered history.

After the *coup-d'état* Napoleon appointed, through the columns of *Le Moniteur* (the government organ), a *Consulting Commission*, composed of eminent men, nine in number, and Montalembert was one of the nine named. He immediately declined ; but, being urged by men of high consideration not to separate himself from the prince-president at this critical juncture, consented to remain upon the commission. Their argument was that what had been done was irreparable ; that France had no other alternative at that moment but of the dictatorship of the "reds" or that of the president *assisted* and *inspired by honest men ;* that it would, moreover, place him in a position favorable for the success of those measures to which he had devoted his life. He proceeded to the Elysée and sounded Napoleon. Though the latter promised nothing, he encouraged every hope. 'Twas then that Montalembert published his letter exhorting the Catholics of France to vote for Napoleon. This letter embodied none of the adulation of the courtier, but was full of honest reserve and caution:

"I neither pretend to *guarantee* the future nor judge the past. . . . To vote for Louis Napoleon is not to approve all he has done; 'tis to choose between him and the total ruin of France. . . . I must urge you to note that I preach neither absolute confidence nor illimited devotion. I do not give myself without reserve to any one. I do not profess any idolatry, neither the idolatry of force of arms nor that of the reason of the people. I am simply for society against socialism; for the *possible* liberty of good against the *certain* liberty of evil; for Catholicism and against revolution."

Foisset, who was Montalembert's life-long friend—the man whom he consulted more than any other, and who may be said to have had the key to his heart, so frank and open was their intercourse—thus criticises his action:

"I have said, even before the fall of the Empire,* that the gravity of such an act could not be denied; yet it should not be exaggerated. On the 12th of December, 1851, Montalembert made the mistake of believing the Socialist party stronger than it was really *after its defeat in the streets of Paris;* he feared too much that the abstention of Catholics from voting on December 20 would have permitted the red element to wreak a revenge which would have been frightful, and he acted as he did in consequence. He was deceived, certainly, as to the danger *at that date;* he was likewise deceived (and still more so) as to the merit of the remedy; Louis Napoleon was much less anti-socialist than our friend believed him

* In the *Life of Père Lacordaire.*

then. . . . But if Montalembert accepted a temporary dictatorship (that which is not incompatible with liberty as the normal state) he did not renounce, as others, the parliamentary régime, he did not insult it; he abstained from every theory affected with *absolutism*. In a word, he made a mistake ; he was not guilty of an apostasy."

His illusion lasted about twenty days. As soon as Napoleon was re-elected he listened to Montalembert with ill-disguised impatience of his counsels. Later, when Napoleon named his senate, he appointed him to a seat, but Montalembert rejected the appointment without a moment's hesitation. No form of solicitation could induce him to accept. He felt that he was wanted as an ornament.* And he was the last man in France to place himself in such an attitude.

The rupture between himself and the Elysée, though in fact dating from this time, did not become public until the announcement was made of the decrees confiscating the property of the house of Orleans. On the day of its announcement he resigned his seat upon that Consulting Committee, which, he said, from the day of its creation had never been consulted.

From this time forward, says Foisset, Charles Montalembert had no other thought but the safeguard of his honor and the preservation of the unity of his life in not allowing to pass an occasion to display his independence and confess with emphasis his political faith. His active career ended with the liberty which expired with the Republic. His eloquence was smothered in the

---

* From a financial standpoint he could but ill afford to decline this doubtful honor. Montalembert was never rich, and the 30,000 francs ($6,000) salary accompanying the seat of senator was a temptation which only makes his refusal the more honorable.

tainted atmosphere of absolutism. Yet he continued to be a member of the House of Deputies down to the year 1857. To some who expressed astonishment that he should have accepted the mandate of the electors of Doubs under the new Empire, after refusing to sit in the senate, he made the very pertinent reply : " Oh ! it can readily happen that the members of the Corps Législatif are but *comparses ;* but with the senators 'tis very different—they are *compères.*"

His last great oratorical success as a public man was on the 22d of June, 1852, in a speech in which he attacked the new constitution, declaring that all serious control upon the part of the legislature was thwarted by the preponderant power of the Council of State. If any argument is needed by an intelligent reader, after the perusal of this constitution, to convince him that it was made for the purpose of giving all control to the president and those of his appointment and to make easy the path to further aggressions, the fact that this constitution was not materially changed by Napoleon when he became emperor should be sufficient. Montalembert's colleagues voted with great enthusiasm the printing of this discourse.* But " the arts of political conversion " made such rapid progress under the Empire that men of Montalembert's free utterance soon ceased to be very welcome. There was less temptation for him to speak, therefore, and little good to be done by his eloquence ; for, as he had said, the legislature was a mere mockery under the present constitution.

* **None** of Montalembert's speeches made after 1852 appear in his works published **in** 1860 and subsequent years. **The** system of repression, carried on by the empire, of all free utterance made **it** impossible **for him to** publish them in France.

VIII.

On the 5th of February, 1852, Montalembert had been received into the French Academy. This honor which his great services had earned for him was witnessed by the largest and most sympathetic auditory since the reception of Royer-Collard (November 13, 1827). He replaced the eminent M. Droz. And, according to the rule governing the admission of new members to the Academy, his discourse was to embrace a sketch of his predecessor. The epoch covered by the life of Droz (1773-1851), the character of his works—the chief being *Histoire du règne de Louis XVI.*, etc.—and his progress from "morality to religion, from reason to faith, from philanthropy to charity, from discussion to authority," defined the field of Montalembert's discourse. It gave him an opportunity to pass in review the history of France from 1789; and, brooding over its pregnant records with the spirit of a man enlightened by study and experience, he produced a philosophical essay rich in crystals of thought and moving in the majesty and elegance of his incomparable diction. His mind was charged with the subject of revolution. He had not only studied it in history, he had seen and contemplated it in actual progression; he had watched its constituent elements drawing together by the law of attraction which governs them, and, when massed in the concrete of revolution, he had seen them explode and scatter destruction.

We know not anywhere a more lucid, condensed, more truly philosophical and comprehensive dissertation upon the great Revolution and the fatal heritage of France therefrom. This discourse and the speech on the *Dotation du Président* (February 10, 1851) constitute a treatise on the political character of France which the student of her history and the seeker after the secret springs of her instability cannot afford to pass by. Uttered by a man who had no political régime to defend, being outside of all party affiliations, whose guiding principles were those which have withstood the test of every change for nearly twenty centuries, there is that condition of mind as a consequence which is the indispensable prerequisite to just and perfect historical judgments.

NOTE.—There hangs in the archiepiscopal residence of Chicago a portrait of Count de Montalembert by Mr. G. P. A. Healey, the eminent artist. The following is a description thereof furnished me at my request by my esteemed friend, Miss Eliza Allen Starr, the author of *Patron Saints* and *Pilgrims and Shrines*— books full of learning, inspired by deep devotion, and adorned in their composition by the double arts of pen and brush. Here are her words :

" This portrait of the great French writer portrays him as he must have been at forty years. But 'tis not the great writer alone, but the orator who is giving forth those wonderful sentences which so thrilled his listeners. The characteristic loftiness of sentiment, the unflinching fidelity to truth, the glow of knightly honor, the delicate irony with which he pierced the consciences of those who had succumbed to the influences of that sceptical period, all are expressed in the pose of the head, the fire of the luminous eyes, the lines of the mobile mouth, around which must have played such varying emotions ; the whole effect intensified by the closely-buttoned coat, as if he had girded himself for one of his grand conflicts with modern indifferentism.

" The picture was painted from life, and Count Auguste de Nauteuil, who saw it in Chicago and whose father had stood shoulder to shoulder with Montalembert in the Chamber of Peers, declared it to be a characteristic likeness.

ST. JOSEPH'S COTTAGE, CHICAGO, ILL.,
299 Huron Street, Nov. 12, 1884."

Part Third.

"Je reste échoué sur le promontoire où m'avait porté le flot des genereuses croyances de mon jeune temps, et je m'y console du naufrage qui m'a préservé de suivre la marée descendante de l'ingratitude et de la peur."

MONTALEMBERT,
Discours, Avant-propos, Tome I.

PART III.

1857–1870.

I.

THE government which sprang into being after the *coup-d'état* was to restore France to material prosperity and to that military prestige which had vanished upon the field of Waterloo. She was to have a constitution without those liberties with which the readers of English and American history associate the idea of constitutional government. That had happened which has been so well described by Burke:

"A system unfavorable to freedom may be so formed as considerably to exalt the grandeur of the state; and men may find in the pride and splendor of prosperity some sort of consolation for the loss of their solid privileges."

It was to be expected that such a government would find in Charles Montalembert an uncompromising opponent. And to the end of his life the imperialism of Napoleon III. was the object of his keenest criticism, both in public and in private. In July, 1853, he wrote to his friend De Lisle on the subject of Napoleon:

". . . I was, as you remember, a decided partisan of Louis Napoleon when he was still an honest man, at war with party intrigues on the one hand and socialist passions on the other; while the *Univers*, with its usual reckless violence, was his decided antagonist and doing its best to identify the Catholic cause with that of the Count de Chambord. I even went very far in my approbation of his *coup-d'état* and its immediate consequences, but I turned away in disgust from the man and his measures as soon as I discovered that he was exclusively directed by mean personal, dynastical motives, and led away by the most inexcusable baseness to commit the crime which triumphant socialism had not dared to commit in 1848, and despoil the house of Orléans, who had twice granted him his life, of their legitimate patrimony. . . . I, for one, both as a Catholic and a Frenchman, shall never resign myself to look upon despotism, silence, and base, material lucre as the *beau idéal* of governments. . . ."

This was always the mistake of the *Univers*—to make the Church dependent upon some dynasty. In 1831 Lacordaire had said in the *Avenir:* "It is not true in any sense that evil is stronger than goodness, and that truth fights upon earth with arms whose inequality demands the succor of absolute power." In 1853, therefore, he whom history had taught that the Church was above and beyond all change, independent of any human government for her existence, felt that she was compromised as far as she could be (in her representative members) when so many of those who should have scorned such a union were endeavoring to link her destiny in France with the lot of an arbitrary and dishonest government. Montalembert's feelings were greatly hurt at the desertion of so many of those who had fought with him the cause of religious and educational freedom. July 19, 1857, he wrote to a friend from Vichy concerning the late elections:

"You will have probably seen in the papers that after twenty-six [continuous] years of public service I have been set aside in the recent elections, and for the first time since I became of age deprived of a vote in the councils of my country; and this thanks to the clergy of Franche-Comté, half of whom voted against me and the other half stayed at home. Such has been the result of the influence of the *Univers* and of its calumnies and denunciations for the last seven years against me and my friends. . . . If they had set up against me a man like Veuillot, or some such, whose opinions they approve of, I should have understood their preferring him; but they have given me up, the oldest and, I think I may say, the stanchest soldier the Church has known in France for many long years, in order to elect an unknown young man who has never done and never will do anything for religion or society, but who belongs to the imperial domesticity and rejoices in wearing a chamberlain's key behind his back. . . ."

II.

It was his delight to escape from the oppressive air of autocracy "to take a bath of life in free England." Her institutions had always had a great attraction for him. When but a young man, as we have seen, the liberal form of her government elicited his praise and his envy. Throughout his public career he cited her, on many occasions, as an active proof of the practicability of religious and educational liberty. In 1855 the result of a visit to this land of his birth was his work *L'Avenir Politique de l'Angleterre* ("The Political Future of England"). An Englishwoman of no ordinary intelligence has said of this book:

"It is wonderfully true and intelligent in its descriptions of English life, society, and modes of thought—descriptions which probably no foreign observer has ever equalled. To compare these brilliant and lifelike sketches with the absurdities given forth by even so well qualified an observer as the last French explorer who has visited our barbarous coasts, the accomplished philosopher, M. Taine, will at once show the reader how infinite was the superiority in knowledge and apprehension of our country and its ways possessed by the noble Frenchman, whose English blood had so strange and enduring an influence upon his life." *

We have not the space to go into an analysis of this book. In fact, it has not been our plan to attempt that task with any of his works.

The *Political Future of England* met everywhere with great success, and especially in England. In five years it passed through six editions in France. In the publisher's preface it is recorded "that the impression produced by this book upon England itself does not appear to lessen; . . . all the reviews and the principal journals take pains daily to develop, contest, or confirm the judgments and previsions of the author; . . . and it has had in addition an honor which, we believe, has never been accorded to any foreign book or writer: it has been the occasion of a debate in the English Parlia-

---

* Mrs. Oliphant's *Memoir of Montalembert*, vol. ii. p. 195 (Tauchnitz).

ment, and, while appealed to on all sides as an authority for the most different opinions, has received unanimous applause."

Three years after the publication of this political work and the journey which was its occasion he returned to England—1858. This trip, like the previous one, resulted in a publication from his pen in the columns of the *Correspondant*—" Un Débat sur l'Inde au Parlement Anglais." " It is the history only," says Mrs. Oliphant, "of a parliamentary debate ; yet so perfectly is the underplay of motive and influence kept before us, and all the side-lights thrown in, that no chapter in history could be more picturesque and no drama more interesting. This is how it appears from an English point of view. From the French its effect was still more striking and noticeable. In every new trait of the freedom and force of English political life, in every detail given and principle laid down, there is a subtle but most powerful contrast, at once melancholy and bitter. . . ." Further on she says : "The contrast between the two nations was carried on with a closeness and keenness which proves how difficult, under the most favorable circumstances, it must be to silence altogether a man of genius and debar him from the subtle and keen-edged weapons which he has always at command."* The entire sketch was republished in the *Times* of London, occupying one whole, vast page, closely printed, of five or six numbers of that paper, in which for almost as many days there was a leading article on the subject of the "Derby," which Montalembert had so admirably described in his sketch—since that event put an inter-

---

* Mrs. Oliphant's *Memoir of Montalembert*, vol. ii. pp. 203, 205.

ruption to, and caused an adjournment of, the debate recounted. The *Times* describes the article with justice as a piece of splendid oratory rather than writing, and its author was treated with great courtesy and warm appreciation.

But the government whose boast was that it rested upon the base of universal suffrage showed its little confidence in the security of its base by seizing the French and English papers reproducing it, and following this up a month later—November, 1858—by a prosecution of Montalembert and the editor of the *Correspondant*. This prosecution was a mistake, as most such prosecutions prove to be when it is too late to withdraw; for it only enabled Montalembert to give a double force to what he had shown in his pamphlet—the deplorable contrast between the liberty of speech allowed in the British Parliament and the smothering restraints placed upon free utterance in the French legislature. The celebrated Dufaure and the illustrious Berryer—the father of the French bar and the greatest lawyer in France—were his advocates. The audience who had collected to hear this trial was "the best and highest that Paris could collect together." The result of the trial in the lower court was a conviction—a fine of three thousand francs and six months' imprisonment for Montalembert, and a month's imprisonment and a fine of a thousand francs for the publisher of the *Correspondant*. Napoleon announced by the *Moniteur* that he remitted the sentence. But Montalembert had appealed the cause to the highest tribunal in the meantime, and, with characteristic independence, refused the remission. The higher court confirmed the sentence, and Napoleon

again pardoned Montalembert. Pending the appeal
Lacordaire wrote to his friend advising him to quit
France for England or Belgium. The **words** of this
saintly Dominican, penned in the simple and austere
retreat which *La Vie intime et religieuse du Père Lacordaire* has so touchingly portrayed, **are** a tribute to the
character of Montalembert which the capable **judgment
of** him who **sent** them and his incapability of flattery
make a valuable piece of evidence. The **letter** is dated
Sorèze, November 26, 1858 : ". . . You **have given** up
your life **to** the establishment in France of an honest
and lawful freedom. You have obtained for us one
liberty which has not yet perished—the liberty of teaching and of education. What, then, remains **to you** but
to suffer for **this cause, which already** owes **you** so
much, and to which **also you owe your greatness**, civil
and religious? . . . God alone knows if **we shall ever
see** better **days, and if France is worthy of** gaining back
in our time **the** institutions which her own **faults have**
lost to her. But whatever may happen in our **time,** the
future will brighten over our graves. It will find us
pure from all treason or defection, from **the *adulation
of success*,** and constant in **our** hope for a state of affairs,
both in religion and politics, which shall be worthy of
that Christianity whose children we **are**. *We have dis-
dained to seek for our faith the support of despotism, wherever it may reign.* We have sought its triumph only by
the means employed by the apostles and martyrs ;* and if
it is to triumph in this world it will be solely by those

---

* **We have** violated Schlegel's dictum—that in good prose every word is under-
lined **and italicized the words** printed so above, that the reader's attention
might be more closely called thereto.

means which gave it the empire over paganism, and which have secured it up to the present time from the hateful conspiracies of false philosophy and false politics.

"Here, my dear friend, is our consolation, and yours in particular. Nothing great was ever exempt from some sensible sign of the cross; the suffering which saved the world is the immortal consecration of all true greatness. You are already affected in your health, and you are about to be so in your safety. In short, you have no longer a country; for that is no country for a man where he is at the mercy of an administration the very laws of which sanction its arbitrary action. . . . You are the honorable victim of it. God, who has given you the love of justice, the sentiment of civil duty, and the still higher comprehension of all liberties, human and divine—God, I say, will give you strength according to your need to endure so many mental evils as well as so many sufferings of the body. I beg of you, above all, not to be bitter against your fate: calm and gentleness are the ornament of suffering. These are what made Jesus Christ so wonderful upon the cross. . . . There can be no doubt that your article was *a protest against the moral degradation of our country*. . . . But this protest exceeded only in a small degree the measure of complaint which an intelligent tyranny permits to the dissatisfied. The absolute silence of thirty-four millions of men is always a reproach in itself. . . I could not have written as you have done, because I am not a political man; but a layman, a former peer of France, might without derogation have given a still sharper edge to his pen. . . ."

If Napoleon or his ministers thought that Montalembert could be frightened into silence by prosecution or bribed to abandon his wonted freedom of utterance by a pardon, they were very much mistaken in their estimate of the man. In October, 1859, he published his article, "Pie IX. et la France en 1849 et en 1859,"* in which Napoleon's well-known betrayal of the cause of the pope to Victor Emmanuel is set forth very strongly. The *Correspondant*, in which it was originally published, and *L'Ami de la Religion*, in which it was reproduced, were each warned by the government. The article, printed in *brochure*, was seized by the government on the 31st of October, and became the object of a judicial pursuit, which terminated by a *nolle prosequi*, the government deeming it advisable not to repeat its former mistake.

The following extracts from Montalembert's letters about this time will define in no mistakable colors his opinion of Napoleon, and also throw light on Montalembert's political views. He is writing in January, 1860: ". . . I am personally fond of the Orléans princes, but I have no sort of faith or confidence in any dynasty or any royalty, past, present, or future. I only love, revere, and desire in the government of this world three things independent of every person—justice, freedom, and honor. These three things are directly antipathetic to Napoleon III. . . . He may be, as you style him, a wonderful politician, if, as is unfortunately the case, enormous lying is one of the principal qualities of great politicians." Later—October, 1867—he said of him: ". . . The base treachery with which he, and he alone,

---

* This will be found in vol. ii. of Montalembert's *Œuvres polémiques et diverses*.

has destroyed the temporal power of the pope will sufficiently stamp his moral character on the judgment of history; while *by the creation of United Italy and United Germany* he has shown *the worthlessness of his policy* and *destroyed that relative greatness of France* which he had received from the hands of the house of Bourbon and the Republic. But, what is worse than all that, he has *debased the moral character of the nation*, and, under the *hollow covering of the material improvements* which you signalize, he has destroyed every principle and every habit of conservative resistance. This will *become evident* in the next revolution, when, instead of the conservative reaction getting the upper hand, as was the case in 1830 and 1848, France will become *a lasting prey* to the atheistical and Jacobinical party which has been fomented in every village by the imperial administration. This you will perhaps see, my dear friend; I trust I shall not, as having lived for sixteen years under the rule of Napoleon III. has utterly disgusted me with this world and everything in it." This was a prediction which events have only too faithfully verified.*

III.

Montalembert's country home was a château of the fifteenth century, called "La Roche en Breny," and was purchased by him in 1842. It is situated among the Burgundian hills, and, because of the similarity of its surroundings to the bleak moorlands of Scotland, his

---

* See in the thirty-fourth volume of the *Catholic World* an article, "Napoleon III. and his Reign," by Rev. Dr. Brann. It is an excellent compend, and will show very clearly why Montalembert and Napoleon could not be otherwise than antagonistic.

friends were accustomed to call him the "laird." But
these features before many years yielded to the artistic
taste of their master. Walks were laid out, skirted with
trees and plants. Groves and orchards were nurtured.
And here he lived to see the acorns which he planted
"shade and pleasant umbrage"; for "how much grows
everywhere, if we but only wait!" exclaims the sadly
poetic Carlyle. Thither from the gayeties of the capi-
tal and the labors and heart-sickenings of public life
he retired to the calm atmosphere of a domestic circle
where he was an idol. Here his heart found rest in the
love of his children, and his spirit got renewed strength
from the writings and the histories of those vigorous
champions of human rights and divine truths whose august procession forms *The Monks of the West.* From
what, in the bitterness of a lofty and sensitive mind,
he has noted as the distinctive notes of the age—"la
faiblesse et la bassesse!"—he turned to the contem-
plation of these men, in whom baseness and weakness
found no place. "I owe to them," he says, "from a
purely human point of view, a great debt for having
reconciled me with men, in opening to my vision a world
where only at distant intervals egotists and liars, the
servile and the ungrateful, darken the path. There I
have known, there have I tasted, that noble independence which belongs to humble souls magnanimous by
their very humility."

IV.

Montalembert's health broke down in 1852. He was
seized by the pangs of a cruel disease which never left

him until his death in 1870. His literary labors during
the remainder of his life were carried on in spite of his
intense suffering. The state of his health made travel
beneficial to him; and *The Monks of the West*, on which
he was more or less actively engaged from 1857, required him to visit libraries not only in France but in
Spain, England, Italy, and other lands. The researches,
however, made for this work extended over many years.
In 1842—in his thirty-second year—when he went to
Madeira, the books he took with him were the Bol-
landist *Acta Sanctorum* and the voluminous records of
the Benedictines. His most laborious researches were
largely made before the *Patrologie* of the Abbé Migne
had made accessible to every considerable library a
complete set of the Doctors and Fathers of the Church.
This fact reveals how irksome must have been in many
instances his search for the book to be consulted before
the labor of consultation (always great enough when the
tome was at hand) had commenced. From these garner-
ings in the rich fields of ancient lore he has enriched
his work with many marginal notes containing passages
of importance from the ancient authors cited, not out
of ostentation of erudition, but to offer some specimens
of the Latin of the middle ages—"of that idiom tem-
pered and transfigured by Christianity. . . . But," he
continues, "I did not possess the courage to reduce
this magnificent language of our ancestors to the feeble
proportions of my own style; I have most always found
my own translation, however literal, so imperfect and un-
faithful that I have wished to give it but as a signboard
by which the reader might find the way to the beauty
and the truth of the originals. . . ." And speaking,

further on, of his care in composition, he says: "The task of the historian so understood resembles that of the graver, who spends his labor, his time, his eyes, who consecrates sometimes ten and twenty years of his life with religious scruple, even to the least details of the brush of the great painter whom his admiration has selected. His pious labor is employed in spreading abroad faithful copies of the model, which he despairs to equal, and thus to make the treasure known only to a few the patrimony of the many."

The Monks of the West[*] was the cherished design of the author's life from his thirty-second year down to the day its last line—leaving it incomplete—was penned in the dim light of an invalid's study. But great books, like great trees, grow slowly and have their roots deep back in the past of the life of him who produces them— whether it be a St. Augustine laboring on his *De Civitate Dei*, to which he had the rare felicity, before the close of a laborious career, of adding the last touch; or a St. Thomas, after years of titanic labor, obliged to see the weakness of the body sinking under the task which an unflagging intellect demanded of it to the last. There is something unspeakably sad in this spectacle of a great artist of the intellect obliged at last to yield his energy of soul to the inherent weakness of its clayey tenement, and after years of devotion, in which, notwithstanding all obstacles, his materials have been garnered, and but a short extension of the lease of life would have been necessary to the completion of the fabric. France in the

---

[*] The best edition of *Les Moines d'Occident* is the octavo one in five vols. The duodecimo in seven vols. is not so full in notes. Both are published by Lecoffre, Paris.

nineteenth century has had **the** misfortune, among her many misfortunes, to see two of her most gifted **sons,** whose genius directed them into the poorly explored fields of history, leaving their work, as the Greek artist left his shield **and** Virgil his *Æneid*, without that rounding touch which **the** architect alone could **have** imparted **to it.** Ozanam and Montalembert were each prevented by death from finishing their works.

The Monks of the West grew out of a plan **which the author had formed of writing a life of** St. Bernard. **He, who had** come, as he himself tells **us, from a** secular **college, with** his mind **almost** a blank **as to the** grand **history of the Christian ages, had** had his interest **quickened into activity by the** revelation of a glorious **past which he found everywhere he travelled, in** the ruins as **well as** the intact architectural remains **of the heroic** days of the Faith. **By** two paths, divergent **for a time,** his mind **was** attracted to these studies. **One was the path of** art, especially architectural, **which** in Montalembert, whose mind was alive to the beautiful under **all forms,** found an ardent and lifelong devotee. **The** other was the path of history (simply), and especially the history of those men who **had left such an** impress everywhere **on the** soil of Europe **and in the histories** of all modern peoples, as he found it and proclaimed **it, as** existing down through the ages for ten centuries.

"The first time," says the author of *The Monks of the West,* "I saw the habit of a monk—shall **I acknowledge it?—it was** upon the boards of **a** theatre, in one of those ignoble **parodies** which **take the place too often** of the pomps **and** solemnities **of religion for modern people.** A few **years afterwards, for the first time, I** encountered a true monk; it was at the foot of the Grande-Chartreuse, at the entrance of that savage gorge, alongside of that bounding torrent, which are never forgotten by any one who visits this celebrated solitude. I did not then know either the services or the glories which this despised frock ought to recall to the mind of the least instructed Christian; but I remember even now the surprise and the emotion which that image caused in my heart."

V.

Protestantism, from the days of Luther down to our own, has systematically misrepresented the history of the Church, with the main object of disestablishing her claim to divine origin and denying her heroic inculcation of the truth which is her heritage. No weapon has been so ruinous in the hands of Protestantism as this system of wholesale vilification. For it has worked both ways in its consequences, not only against the Church but against Protestantism's self, opening, in its but too poorly constructed ramparts, breaches upon all sides for the entrance of scepticism, rationalism, materialism. Protestantism, in its dissension, having taken with it but a small segment of the perfect circle of revealed truth, has proven itself, at the rear and on both flanks, lamentably pregnable to the weapons of modern unbelief, which, first nourished in its citadel, has passed out with the easy secrets of its weakness, only to turn upon it and destroy it. This attitude of Protestantism has had the effect of enlisting the energies of the scholars of the Church in the fields of patristic and mediæval history. Many of the more enlightened of Protestant scholars,* seeing the disastrous trend of this warfare, have devoted their talents to rescuing the history of the early ages from the obscurity with which the detritus of time and the calumnies of false historians have covered it.

As his contribution to the cause of the truth Montalembert designed writing a life of St. Bernard. The researches made with this design revealed to him the glory of the past which had preceded that saint, and of which he was but an outgrowth.† He found that he was especially an outgrowth of monasticism—a fact not sufficiently appreciated and emphasized by his biographers. He found, too, that great monks had filled Christendom with their voice before Bernard. That sense of justice, ever a striking feature of his character, would not permit him to pass in silence over the record of these men. The chivalrous sentiment which had attracted him into the lists of history as the champion of the maligned cause of Bernard induced him to become the champion of the cause of monasticism itself. Notwithstanding the immense labor which this design must have foreshadowed to a man with heavy political duties resting upon him, he did not shrink from the

---

* Notably the Protestant Guizot. We need scarcely recall, as a feature of this great movement and its results, the patristic studies of which Cardinal Newman and other eminent Englishmen—before their conversion—were the authors, and which were the main instrument of their conversion. A like movement took place in Germany with like results, represented by such scholars as Von Müller, Voigt, Leo, Hurter, and the two Menzels. "This work," says the author of *The Monks of the West*, "so indispensable to the honor and the vindication of Catholicism, was commenced by Protestants, by indifferentists, and in some instances by declared adversaries."

† *Les Moines d'Occident*, Introduction, p. vii.

enterprise, devoting to it all his *subseciva tempora*. The change involved, too, the sacrifice of many pages ready for publication—some five hundred in number—which had to be entirely recast. From an artistic point of view he felt, too, that his original plan must suffer by the alteration which he proposed in it—for it was still to St. Bernard as the culminating-point of his design that his labors were directed. But this could not discourage even one of his fine artistic tastes. The reason he gives is worthy of the man: "There is for every Christian a beauty higher than art—the beauty of truth."* Had this work been published before, he says, "it might, as did the *Histoire de Sainte Élisabeth* twenty-five years ago, have opened a new pathway across the vast field of Catholic history. Now it can only hope to mark a place in the series of contemporary studies. The subject, heretofore completely ignored and forgotten, has since been approached by many. Although nothing considerable has yet been attempted upon the subject of monasticism in its *ensemble*, the ground of this subject has been sufficiently dug over by monographs, as detailed as numerous, to have fatigued in a measure the public interest, and to make it difficult to fix the attention of the reader upon ground so well known and pathways so well cleared. On that account alone many results reached by me through laborious researches will not be held as discoveries and will scarcely fix the attention of the curious."

It is unnecessary to say that the judgment of those

---

* "Mais il y a pour tout chrétien une beauté supérieure à l'art, la beauté de la verité."

who were competent to judge has not assented to this conclusion of self-depreciation. The work may have fallen short—as all, especially the greatest, works do—of the lofty prototype formed in the author's mind. This book, which has made the author's own (in the language of an ancient) the province of history which it invades, might still have been more than it is if the urgent cares of politics had not relegated its composition to a period when disease had made all sustained labor not only painful but almost impossible. Yet the work was pushed ahead with true heroism. "Shall I ever," he said, "be able to finish it? All I can say is that I have done my utmost. But this utmost is very little. I cannot stay out of bed more than an hour or two every day; and when I have written a page, or even half a page, I feel quite exhausted." No reader, in following the majestic, the graceful march of this history, giving evidence on every page of deep and far-reaching investigation, would suspect that it was completed under circumstances almost incompatible with composition.

In 1858 Cardinal Newman, in considering the want which *The Monks of the West* has been written to supply, and contemplating the poetry, the heroism, the sorrows, the earnest labors, the rude trials—all the varied features of monasticism—concluded that none other than a Christian Virgil could do justice to a subject so surcharged with the materials of epic and bucolic verse, redolent of so much sweetness, affection, devotion, beauty, innocence, kindliness, simplicity, and abounding in bravery, in hardihood, in honor, in suffering.

"... How could he have brought out the poetry of those simple laborers, who has told us of that old man's flowers and fruits, and of the satisfaction, as a king's, which he felt in those innocent riches! He who had so huge a dislike of cities, and great houses, and high society, and sumptuous banqueting, and the canvass for office, and the hard law, and the noisy lawyer, and the statesman's harangue; he who thought the country proprietor as even too blessed, did he but know his blessedness, and who loved the valley, winding stream, and wood, and the hidden life which they offer and the deep lessons which they whisper—how could he have illustrated that wonderful union of prayer, penance, toil, and literary work, the true *otium cum dignitate*, a fruitful leisure and a meek-hearted dignity, which is exemplified in the Benedictine! ..."

Has Montalembert realized this wish—has he proved to be that Christian Virgil which the then priest of the Oratory (the now cardinal) longed for? He has surely gone far towards doing so. Though he could brave the din of popular assemblies, he loved not less the sweet repose of the woods and the fields; though duty held him much among the crowded dwelling-places of men, where sin and misery, pride and pomp, are mingled to offend the eye and hurt the heart, that retirement which is removed—yet not in disdain nor pride nor misanthropy—from all this was dear to him. The book itself is a witness of these assertions. Where will we find poetry, if not in Montalembert's chapters, "The Happiness of the Cloister," "Ruin," "The Monks and Nature"? And yet let not the reader think that *The Monks of the West* was written in a spirit of insane admiration, of indiscriminate praise; that he will find there "the impure sacrifice of a lie." To assure him on this score he will meet at the very threshold, in the author's magnificent introduction, a chapter entitled "Relâchement." Or let him read the work in its entirety, and he will find in their proper place irregularities mentioned and condemned as they occurred. "I will recount these abuses," he says. "But from what source? From the very monks themselves. For in the majority of instances it is from them alone that we have our information; it is to their avowals, their complaints, their recitals, to the chronicles of their houses written by themselves with a freedom and a simplicity more admirable even than their laborious patience. They did not know the rule dictated by the prophet of their persecutors: *Lie with hardihood, lie ever.* They spoke the whole truth and at their own cost; they spoke it with sorrow, blushing when they did it, but with the well-founded certainty that the evil which they denounced to posterity, very far from being the natural result of their institution, was a direct contradiction of it."

Yet the critical reader of Montalembert's great book will not find it characterized by that clear and steady light so pre-eminently distinctive of the genius of that cardinal whom we have just quoted. The acumen of the latter, his delicate touch, his mild force and freedom from headlong enthusiasm, are absent from the pages of the devout and eloquent peer. Newman in his page suggests the mild glow of an autumn day, under whose effulgence everything wears an air of peace and satisfaction, when the leaves of the bough gently stir, the birds complacently sing and move leisurely from tree to tree, the smoke up-curls majestically in twisted columns, and the air is fragrant from the last flowers of the year. Montalembert's page is the sky of April, where clouds gather, thunder rolls, lightning flashes, and the sun comes out anon to dazzle us with its splendor. Nor had Montalembert the genius of Ozanam, which bears a close resemblance to that of Newman, and which some will pronounce superior to both the peer's and the cardinal's when the trio are considered in the character of historians. But if Montalembert's occupation forbade not his being surpassed by any of his contemporaries as an historian, as he was unsurpassed by any as an orator, yet when we seek standards of comparison we must select of his contemporaries one who had the rare homage of a posthumous crown from the mixed conclave of a French Academy, and another who, by a life of uninterrupted study and quiet, as well as by an edifying sanctity and sweetness of character, has attained the cardinalate and the general praise of his countrymen, without regard to creed, as a good man and a great scholar.

Montalembert's power lay chiefly in masterful statement, varied by indignation, or irony, or pity, or pathos. His pages are marked by majesty and grace, and lofty and varied utterance. He had the industry and the learning adequate to his subject. But he threw it into the mould of oratory, consciously or unconsciously, wittingly or unwittingly. *The Monks of the West*, varied as it is by the gifts of his pen, the patience of his research, is really nothing else than an historical philippic in many portions. He is soaring always.

And we tire sometimes in being ever on the wing. But this is not said in detraction. Nor does it materially detract. For the truth and the beauty, and the power of these two, are all there. Hence is it that these volumes have become so popular, have found so wide an audience. And they must long remain for the student to whom the period embraced by these volumes is unknown, because of their rich freight of facts and references, a safe guide along that dangerous pathway where so many have gone astray or found pitfalls.

And they are far from deserving a hostile criticism made by Sainte-Beuve, who, after he had become one of the sycophants of the new empire, smarted under the flail of Montalembert's criticism. This critic affects to see in the pages of the *Monks of the West* nothing critical —nothing of that pith and marrow characteristic of the books which live and which are the production of thought, of experience, of a fair and indulgent temper; hence that there is the lack of that individuality, or rather *originality*, which stamps even an old subject which has filtered anew through a vigorous and acute mind. And in his fondness for that species of criticism Sainte-Beuve goes so far as to charge both Lacordaire and Montalembert of having drawn all their inspiration from their old comrade, Lamennais. "To resume," he says, "Montalembert is, after all, but a soldier; he is such in everything and throughout; as such he will leave in the history of the political and religious contests of his time a luminous trace: Lacordaire and he, only *two lieutenants* of Lamennais after all, who have brilliantly continued the campaign after *their general* had passed over to the enemy. But the great deserter, even in his absence, rules and dominates (*les domine*) them and remains present to their thought, to the thought of each : they are *only first lieutenants* after all." *

The chosen fields of Montalembert's labors with pen and voice lay in that province where many masterminds preceding him, who were not deluded by false philosophy or the petty guides of self-interest, have established their fame and their claims upon the gratitude of mankind. Hence it is that when we come to compare Montalembert with men who, with abilities and principles akin to his, stood in the same general relations to society, a striking similarity of action will likely present itself. Hence, up to his change, he may resemble Lamennais, as he certainly does resemble Burke, and others who might be named. A bigoted and an angered critic might conclude that he was a mere copyist from this fact. But in every sphere, among men of eminence therein, the same phenomenon presents itself. And it should not provoke astonishment. For the principles of Truth, as the principles of Error, are still the same, and produce results which, in the long run, differ only in degree. He who works in the cause of Truth works out of love for Truth. His labors will not be ranked with those brilliant aberrations of deluded geniuses who have dazzled while they deluded the world. He cannot hope, whatever the coloring of fancy, or the polish of varied study, or the possession of a vigorous judgment may do (and they will do a very great deal, for they will give freshness and grace and the power of conviction to his narrative), that his labors shall be more than an extension of those old grooves which the

* Sainte-Beuve, *Portraits Contemporains*, Paris, 1882, tome ii. p. 442.

champions of Truth in the past wore so deeply in their day, and in which alone humanity has travelled with safety as upon the only highway to the stable and the good. There is nothing essentially new in this world; what appears to be newness, whether on the side of Truth or Error, is only a difference in form and in degree. He who writes to-day upon the principles of government is only recasting, under the forms of a passing fashion, that which others may have done in the fashion and with the advantages of their day, as well in the last century or in any that have preceded it. The same in the realms of religious thought or in that secular record of the longings and doubts and fancies of different peoples—in literature. He is only unweaving the threads of another weaver, more or less skilled than himself, to make a fabric of a different figure of the same fundamental materials. And historical composition is only original by virtue of its garb, its arrangement, its display of erudition, and the results of a tireless energy in garnering which it receives from its author; the facts, which are its fundamentals, are not the creation of the historian. If this be true of the intellectual world, it is also true of the natural. Nature herself does the same thing; her originality is but the originality of variating forms. The leaves of the forest, which hang so lightly from their delicate supports, have drawn their essence from the mould made of other leaves and plants which grew in another age for the delight of other eyes and the umbrage of other heads.

VI.

Montalembert's last appearance as an orator—the last time he raised his voice to speak with that freedom which is essential to the utterance of a man of his character—was in 1863 on the free soil of Belgium, at the great religious meeting known as the Congress of Malines. The feebleness of his health obliged him to deliver his address seated. "For four hours," says a spectator, "the illustrious orator held captive an assembly of nearly four thousand persons by his penetrating, elevated, and powerful address, and which drew from it enthusiastic acclamations and frantic applauses. We have beheld a veritable miracle of human eloquence." His audience was a lofty one; it contained cardinals, bishops, high dignitaries of Church and state—the foremost class of Catholics from many lands. The subject was the relation of the Church to the modern world. And no phase of modern society appeared to the orator's judgment so important, because so large, so powerful, so imminent, as the spread of democracy. "For my part I am no democrat; but I am less an absolutist. I endeavor above all not to be blind. Full of deference and love for the past in all that is good and great in it, I do not despise the present and I study the future. Looking on in advance, I see nothing anywhere but democracy. I see this deluge rise—rise continually—reaching everything and overflowing everything. I fear it as a man, but as a Christian I do not fear it; for where I see the deluge I see also the ark. Upon that great ocean of democracy, with its abysses, its whirlpools, its breakers, its dead calms, and its hurricanes, the Church alone may venture forth without defiance and without fear. She alone will never be swallowed up there. She alone has a compass which never varies and a Pilot who makes no mistakes."

This subject of universal democracy is said to have embittered to some extent Montalembert's days. Certain it is that the student of his writings and his speeches meets everywhere with the outcroppings of this deep stratum of thought, and everywhere it appears impressive and solemn.

VII.

Montalembert's pen was never more prolific, never more versatile, than in this last period of his life, from 1857 to 1870. Everything he has written is marked by the same high art of finish, the same depth of thought; because whatever he attempted to do he did conscientiously, massing everything he could collect upon the subject to be handled, arranging and digesting, and not until his material had passed through the machinery of long and careful thought putting his pen to paper. He has written on many subjects and produced masterpieces in each class. Art, biography, literature, history, political controversy, political manifestoes have all engaged his pen. In the province of political controversy we have his *Political Future of England*, already mentioned; his *Victory of the North in the United States*, which has been called a hymn of triumph over that success; many letters published from time to time, and

---

* See this address published under the title *L'Église libre dans l'État libre*. This title embodies the ideal of Montalembert's **politics**.

which are collected in his works; finally, his admirably trenchant letters to Cavour in 1860 and 1861. We know of nothing outside of his speeches which surpasses in rapidity and strength his flaying arraignment of the hero of Italian centralization. In them we hear the echo of those noble political sentiments which will embalm his *discours*, and the unchanging devotion to which, in all the truckling measures of expediency going on around him, enabled him to adopt as the motto of his works, when he began their publication in uniform volumes, the phrase which is a proud one for a man who has been long engaged in the highest questions and in the highest positions of politics—*Qualis ab incepto*. Here we discover all the old filial tenderness of soul which blazed in such splendor in the speech on the Roman expedition. Having visited Poland and Hungary in 1861, he gathered many materials for a work upon the latter country, which were found arranged and in order after his death. Returning to France, he published on Poland his article, "A Nation in Mourning"—one of the most pathetic pieces of writing which ever came from his pen. "It is a poem rather than an article," has said an appreciative critic, "but its lofty poetic strain, its touching and highly colored pictures, its lyrical outbursts of translated song, mark its true character even more clearly than versification could have done. Poland had been the first object of Montalembert's interest. She had always kept a foremost place in his affections. The aspect of this mourning nation awoke in his mind nothing but the profoundest emotion. Her piety, her struggles for national existence, her long and heroic perseverance and many misfortunes, roused him into a very passion of pity and sympathy." Finally, there remains to mention his beautiful *Life of Lacordaire*, which is a model composition of its kind. The grace of the style, the sweetness of the sentiment which it breathes, the close and intimate view which it gives us of the illustrious preacher, the treasures in the way of extracts from Lacordaire's letters to Montalembert, give this composition a charm which does not attach in the same degree to anything else which he has written.

VIII.

Towards the end of his life an event occurred in his household which, though it was sudden, should not have been unlooked for. His youngest daughter, a brilliant girl, who possessed "much of her father's talent and many of his characteristics, who had made a brilliant entry into 'the world' some time before, announced her desire to become a nun." "One day," says M. Cochin, "his charming and beloved child entered that library which all his friends know so well, and said to him : ' I am fond of everything around me. I love pleasure, wit, society and its amusements ; I love my family, my studies, my companions, my youth, my life, my country; but I love God better than all, and I desire to give myself to him.' And when he said to her, ' My child, is there something which grieves you ?' she went to the book-shelves and sought out one of the volumes of *The Monks of the West*. ' It is you,' she answered, ' who have taught me that withered hearts and weary souls are not the things which we ought to offer to God.'" Could pen have pictured a sweeter picture, or the imagination have conceived a day of purer recompense for the author of volumes consecrated to humility and heroism? "Some days after," continues the same sympathetic narrator, "I had the happiness of accompanying the family to the humble sanctuary where the marriage ceremony was to take place; the priest was at the altar to celebrate the bridal, and the bride, adorned for her marriage, in her orange-flowers and bridal veil, knelt radiant and tender at the altar. But there was no bridegroom there. The bridegroom was that invisible Husband who for two thousand years has attached so many young souls to him by bonds which cannot be broken, and drawn them by a charm which nothing can equal." The reader, if he has perused *The Monks of the West*, has read, at the conclusion of one of the volumes treating of the Anglo-Saxon saints, what Mrs. Oliphant calls "one of the most affecting utterances of suppressed emotion which perhaps has ever been put upon record." It is a description of this episode.

This daughter was the favorite of Montalembert. She was the youngest of three—he never had a son. His favorite appellation in addressing her was, "Mon bonheur." It was a sacrifice to part with her—a sacrifice whose keenness only a parent can appreciate. His health was poor, his days were numbered, and the sweet ministrations of this dear child would have made any one less human than Montalembert exclaim that she had left him to his great regret—*à ma grande désolation!* But this natural sorrow soon gave way to a deep and genuine joy that this tender scion had found a safe asylum for her innocence, where she would be happy and useful, free from the sorrows of the outer world. The time, too, for his leaving that world was, as we have intimated, approaching rapidly. Soon society had to be given up. Then came the arm-chair. From 1867 his suffering continued to be very acute down to the day of his death. Then the easy-chair had to be abandoned for the bed. Mrs. Oliphant, who knew him in these waning days, has devoted many pages of beauty and pathos to their memory. "Never," says she, "was there a more striking evidence of that vigor and life of the soul which is independent of—nay, almost in antagonism with—the strength of the body. . . . Death had nothing to do with such a man. Looking at him, the spectator felt it to be of all things the least credible. He was an embodied contradiction to that condition of humanity, an assertion of immortality more triumphant than any argument. Physicians might say what they would, we believe that no one could have seen Montalembert in that prolonged and most painful passage out of life without feeling a half-indignant, half-contemptuous inclination to deny the possibility of dying. With such a deathless, brave, bright, and unconquerable individuality death had nothing to do."

It was while he lay upon his bed of pain that the question of Papal Infallibility was taken up for discussion. His attitude towards this question has been the occasion for some of the same religious faith, but not of the same politics, to misrepresent Montalembert. Others have even gone so far as to say that he died in schism, because they would have rejoiced in

seeing so valiant a soldier of the Church which they
despised guilty of defection in his last days. Montalembert felt very deeply upon the question, and made
the mistake—because he was but a layman—of publish-
ing a letter upon the subject in the *Gazette of France*,
February 28, 1870. Foisset says that Montalembert did
not oppose the declaration of the dogma, *except as inop-
portune*. It was not that the doctrine of the infallibility
of the pope was repugnant to him, but he had very grave
apprehensions as to the use which might be made of the
pontifical prerogative against the political ideas which
were dear to him. Fundamentally his fidelity to the
Church was in nowise affected. As the council approached he wrote to a friend—Lady Herbert: "I am
in opposition as strongly as it is permissible; but I
am firmly resolved, whatever happens and whatever it
may cost me, never to pass the inviolable limits. . . .
The Church is none the less for me the Church—that
is to say, the sole repository of truth and of virtue,
which are at the same time the most necessary and
the most difficult of access for modern society. She
has more than ever (and she alone has) the key of two
great mysteries of human life—of sorrow and of sin.
Therefore I feel myself penetrated with a tenderness
for her and a respect which have only augmented with
age. At the age of sixty, which I shall soon attain, I
feel that I love her and believe in her with an energy
very different from that of my twentieth year. . . . Being unable any more to serve her here, I will preserve
at least, down to the day when her last succors shall
come to sweeten the end of my too long sufferings—I
will preserve for her a soul more than ever docile to

her sublime teachings, more than ever desirous of her supernatural consolations, more than ever in love with her divine beauty."

Three or four weeks before his death he said: "What is repugnant to me is not the infallibility of the pope in matters of faith; it is his omnipotence over political questions, which certain exaggerated spirits will seek to erect into a dogma as a sequence of the doctrinal infallibility of the Holy See." And when some one asked him what he would do if infallibility were proclaimed, he raised himself in his sick-chair and with an animated gesture exclaimed: "Are we not told that the pope is a father? Very well, then; fathers sometimes wish us to do that which is not conformable to our ideas. In such a case the son struggles to persuade his father; he discusses with him. But if he see it is useless to argue he submits. *I shall do the same.*" The person replied: "Oh! you will submit exteriorly. But how will you reconcile this submission with your convictions?" He replied with more emphasis than before: "I will make no attempt to reconcile them. I will submit my will, as we submit in other matters of faith. And God does not ask me to understand; he asks me to submit my intelligence and my will, *and I shall submit them.*"

Near his Paris home, where he died, was the old church of St. Thomas of Aquin. Here he succeeded, by an expenditure of much exertion, in hearing his last Mass and receiving communion. He soon became so weak that only an occasional letter could be written. The night before his death he was writing a letter to Dr. Newman, and while it was but half-finished fell asleep over it. Shortly before that he had finished some notes of criticism and admiration to Baron Hübner upon his *Life of Sixtus the Fifth*. On this evening of the day preceding his demise, March 12, 1870, he wrote these words to the author of that work: "You have understood and judged the great Catholic reaction of the second half of the sixteenth century with a wisdom and impartiality for which I thank you, in the first place, as a Christian, and on which I congratulate you as being myself a publicist and also a historian, though of an age more distant and forgotten than that which you have made to live again. You have not concealed either the shadows or the stains which are inseparable from the human element which is always so visible and so powerful in the Church; and even by this means you bring out all the more clearly the divine element which always prevails in the end, and consoles us by flooding everything with its gentle and convincing light."

The next morning he awakened refreshed. But a sudden paroxysm of pain alarmed his attendants. The priest came in time to administer Extreme Unction. His death was without pain, as is frequently the case in long illnesses. He prayed until consciousness left him. He was buried, at his own desire, "in the hallowed ground of the Picpus convent, where lie the victims of the Revolution, where only those who are descended from those victims or connected with them can lie." He had this privilege by right of his wife. "He chose his last rest there beside the *unfortunate*—by those who had perished either for the sake of religion or for their honorable adherence to a fallen cause."

Foisset was the man above all others who should have written the biography of Charles Montalembert; for biography is a task which belongs especially to friendly hands. Whilst Montalembert's youthful ardor was kindling at the hearth of those artistic studies which ever after occupied so large a space in his intellectual horizon, he heard through Lacordaire of certain letters, "full of grave observations and prudent counsels," which he was in the habit of receiving from a bosom friend and former schoolfellow at the law-school of Dijon. So he became acquainted with Foisset through the good offices of their common friend. The friendship started from a correspondence in 1837, which Montalembert began. Foisset was then a judge in the Côte-d'Or. He was forty and Montalembert was twenty-seven. A man of firm and excellent judgment, which had been matured and strengthened by study, he was held, by the duties of his profession, in a provincial town, a distant spectator of events upon the great stage of central activity, where, if circumstances had been favorable, his abilities would have made him a central figure.

Their meeting has been described by one who heard it from the lips of Montalembert, who loved to repeat it. "The visit," says M. Douhaire, "which Montalembert had promised to his new friend did not take place until the following year [1838]. It was an evening in autumn, when M. Foisset, then near Beaune, perceived before his door the arrival, in a simple hired conveyance, of the even then celebrated representative of the Catholic interests in the Chamber of Peers. The surprise was great on both sides. The brilliant *collaborateur* of the *Avenir*, the hardy founder and eloquent defender of the Free School (*l'École libre*), the orator so favorably heard at the Luxembourg, astonished the grave magistrate by his juvenile air. And, from his side, the provincial judge deceived the expectations of his Parisian visitor by the extent and variety of his learning, the superiority and correctness of his views upon passing events, and upon those of religion in particular, nor least of all by the lively sympathy which he gave evidence of and with which he inspired at the same time. The young peer (he afterwards confessed it with a smile) had expected to meet, if not a provincial Robin crammed with practical jurisprudence and local erudition, at least a man cantoned in a certain order of ideas and closely tied to some political party, as is so often the case in the provinces. But he found himself face to face with *un esprit d'élite*—a superior character—less occupied with the law than with the prophets, at home on all questions, speaking of philosophy, literature, politics, and religion like a man who had his own ideas on each subject and knew how to defend them. . . . He was rather below Montalembert in height, and of somewhat irregular stature, his forehead resembling those of antique busts, his expression of countenance sweet, his smile refined and benevolent, which did not unsettle the previsions of the visitor, though he afterwards confessed to being somewhat disconcerted by this first interview."*

The correspondence which had opened their friend-

* Introduction par M. P. Douhaire dans *Le Comte de Montalembert*, par M. Th. Foisset. Paris, 1877.

ship, strengthened in its motives by the results of this first interview, continued throughout Montalembert's life with a great and unflagging activity. In these letters the friends disclosed each to each all their plans, and received in return the advice, the criticism, the objections of the other, together with that encouragement which is one of friendship's choicest fruits. Foisset, as a man upon whose head he could rely, was called upon for his judgment relative to almost every speech, every composition, planned by Montalembert. Foisset in his turn, as years and experience whitened the hair and developed the judgment of the peer, called upon him for like services; so that not a line, we are told, of the *Vie du P. Lacordaire** was printed until it had passed under the eyes of Montalembert.

This acquaintance was a lasting boon, especially to the younger man. For who has ever experienced the services of a judicious friend, under circumstances such as Montalembert so often found himself in—when the mind oppressed by a mass of details, and the judgment wavering over the correctness of its action, has had this kindly light, this genial aid, this superadded strength to clear, to guide, to lift the judgment to a proper elevation of standpoint—who has ever had this invaluable succor but will appreciate it in the case of the young peer? This want, too, is felt the more the higher a man ascends the scale of responsibility. And that a man with duties in a high sphere has availed himself of this aid is not derogatory of his judgment, but rather the reverse of derogatory.† But Foisset followed Mon-

---

* By Foisset.
† "Certain it is that whosoever hath his mind fraught with many thoughts

talembert in a few years to the **grave, and before he could perform the task which** his unequalled advantages would have **enabled** him **to** perform as the **intimate friend of** thirty-three years and **the** possessor **of a** correspondence embracing that period, **which, now that he,** too, **has gone, will never** see the light.

He did **leave a** biographical sketch **of his friend, which,** notwithstanding that **it is incomplete, "is the** most authoritative we have **concerning the life, the character, and** the **spirit** of **the labors of the eminent man to** whom its pages **are devoted."** It was published originally in the *Correspondant* in 1872; and the **author of the present sketch has been governed throughout by it in forming his** judgments **of doubtful questions, made so by the** meagreness **or obscurity of the evidence.**

Of the *Memoir of Montalembert* by **Mrs. Oliphant we must** say **a few words. It has much in it that is delicate and exquisite—what we should** expect from **one of Mrs.** Oliphant's skill **as a writer of** English. **But it reads more like a** romance **than a sober biography. This may** make **it** acceptable **to the palates of novel-lovers, but** it **palls upon** palates accustomed **to** stronger **food.** Mrs. **Oliphant is** a novelist, **and she** did **not dismiss her** art **in writing of** Montalembert. The **temptation to** high seasoning **of sentiment has not been resisted. The impression, therefore, left by her book is more** painful

---

his wits **and** understanding do **clarify and break** up in the communicating and discoursing with another: he **tosseth his** thoughts more easily ; he marshalleth them more orderly ; he seeth **how they** look when they **are** turned into words ; finally, **he** waxeth wiser than himself, and that more by an hour's discourse than a day's meditation. . . . For friendship maketh indeed **a** fair day **in the affections,** from storm and tempests ; **but it maketh** daylight **in the understanding, out of** darkness and confusion **of thoughts"** (Lord Bacon, twenty-seventh Essay).

than pleasant. It is that exquisite sense of melancholy, of pleasurable pain, which successful novels produce. Such an effect is unhealthy, and it is unjust to draw it from so real, so earnest, so healthy a career as Montalembert's, of which intelligent conviction and not romance was the guiding spirit.

www.ingramcontent.com/pod-product-compliance
Lightning Source LLC
Chambersburg PA
CBHW021942160426
43195CB00011B/1191